BLOODAXE CONTEMPORARY

Throughout the twentieth century, France has been a dominant force in the development of European culture. It has made essential contributions and advances not just in literature but in all the arts, from the novel to film and philosophy; in drama (Theatre of the Absurd), art (Cubism and Surrealism) and literary theory (Structuralism and Post-Structuralism). These very different art forms and intellectual modes find a dynamic meeting-point in post-war French poetry.

Some French poets are absorbed by the latest developments in philosophy or psychoanalysis. Others explore relations between poetry and painting, between the written word and the visual image. There are some whose poetry is rooted in Catholicism, and others who have remained faithful to Surrealism, and whose poetry is bound to a life of action or political commitment.

Because it shows contemporary French poetry in a broader context, this new series will appeal both to poetry readers and to anyone with an interest in French culture and intellectual life. The books themselves also provide an imaginative and exciting approach to French poets which makes them ideal study texts for schools, colleges and universities.

Each volume is a single, unabridged collection of poems presented in a parallel-text format, with the French text facing an English verse translation by a distinguished expert or poet-translator. The editor of each book is an authority on the particular writer, and in each case the editor's introduction presents not only a critical appreciation of the work and its place in the author's output but also a comprehensive account of its social, intellectual and cultural background.

The series itself has been planned in such a way that the individual volumes will build up into a stimulating and informative introduction to contemporary French poetry, giving readers both an intimate experience of how French poets think and write, and a working overview of what makes poetry important in France.

BLOODAXE CONTEMPORARY FRENCH POETS

Series Editors: Timothy Mathews & Michael Worton

Timothy Mathews is Professor of French at University College London. His books include *Reading Apollinaire: Theories of Poetic Language* (Manchester University Press, 1987 & 1990) and *Literature, Art and the Pursuit of Decay in 20th Century France* (CUP, 2000). He co-edited *Tradition, Translation, Trauma: The Classic and the Modern* (OUP, 2011) with Jan Parker, and co-translated Luce Irigaray's *Prières quotidiennes/Everyday Prayers* (Larose/University of Nottingham Press, 2004) with Irigaray. The first volume in this series, *On the Motion and Immobility of Douve* by Yves Bonnefoy, has an introduction by him.

Michael Worton was Vice-Provost and Fielden Professor of French Language and Literature at University College London. He has published extensively on contemporary French writers, with two books on Michel Tournier, and co-edited *Intertextuality* (1990), *Textuality and Sexuality* (1993), *Women's Writing in Contemporary France* (2003), *National Healths: Gender, Sexuality and Health in a Cross-Cultural Context* (2004), *Liberating Learning* (2010) and *French Studies in and for the 21st Century* (2011). The second volume in the Bloodaxe Contemporary French Poets series, *The Dawn Breakers* by René Char, is introduced and translated by him.

BLOODAXE CONTEMPORARY FRENCH POETS: 2

RENÉ CHAR

The Dawn Breakers

Les Matinaux

Translated & introduced by
MICHAEL WORTON

BLOODAXE BOOKS

BLOODAXE CONTEMPORARY FRENCH POETS: 2
René Char: *The Dawn Breakers*

Original French text of *Les Matinaux*
by René Char © Éditions Gallimard 1950.
English translation and Introduction © Michael Worton 1992.

ISBN: 978 1 85224 133 9

This edition published 1992 by
Bloodaxe Books Ltd,
Eastburn,
South Park,
Hexham,
Northumberland NE46 1BS.

www.bloodaxebooks.com
For further information about Bloodaxe titles
please visit our website and join our mailing list
or write to the above address for a catalogue.

Supported using public funding by
**ARTS COUNCIL
ENGLAND**

Bloodaxe Books Ltd and Michael Worton wish
to thank the Ministère de la Culture, Paris,
and the Department of French, the University of Cambridge,
for help given towards translation and production costs.

Digital reprint of the 1992 edition

CONTENTS

Les Matinaux

The Dawn Breakers

GENERAL EDITORS' PREFACE

The Bloodaxe Contemporary French Poets series aims to bring a broad range of post-war French poetry to as wide an English-speaking readership as possible, and it has specific features which are designed to further this aim.

First of all, each volume is devoted to a complete, unabridged work by a poet. This is designed to maintain the coherence of what a poet is trying to achieve in publishing a book of poems. We hope that in this way, the particular sense of a poet working within language will be highlighted. Secondly, each work appears in parallel translation. Finally, each work is prefaced by a substantial essay which gives a critical appreciation of the book of poetry, of its place in its author's work, as well as an account of its social and intellectual context.

In each case, this essay is written by an established critic with a love of French poetry. It aims not only to be informative, but also to respond in a lively and distinctive way to the pleasures and challenges of reading each poet. Similarly, the translators, often poets in their own right, adopt a range of different approaches, and in every case they seek out an English that gives voice to the uniqueness of the French poems.

Each translation in the series is not just faithful to the original, but aims to recreate the poet's voice or its nearest equivalent in another language: each is a translation from French poetry into English poetry. Each essay seeks to make its own statement about how and why we read poetry and think poetry. The work of each poet dovetails with others in the series to produce a living illustration of the importance of poetry in contemporary French culture.

TIMOTHY MATHEWS,
MICHAEL WORTON,
University College London

INTRODUCTION

René Char (1907-88) is often described as a poet of nostalgia who is essentially concerned with his own childhood in Provence and with the pre-industrial and pre-nuclear world. His poems have also often been described as hermetic, as "difficult" or "intellectual". Internationally recognised as one of the most important French poets since the Surrealists, perhaps even since Paul Valéry, he is respected as a poet-philosopher but he has never become a popular poet. This says much about what many modern, urban readers expect from contemporary poetry: they want to encounter both familiar, "relevant" images and a language which corresponds to what they know and speak, hence the commercial success of such different poets as Prévert, Brel, Betjeman and Larkin.

Char does not seek to please his readers but to make them more aware of their own lives, and this he does by capturing and crystallising brief moments of existence which may aid readers to understand their own experiences. However, his imagery is drawn from a direct and sustained contact with Nature in Provence, a region which most of his readers will not know at all or will know only as tourists rushing from one celebrated site to another. And yet when we discover in the poetry reference to Vaucluse villages or sites such as Le Thor, Maussane, Thouzon, Les Dentelles de Montmirail, the Fontaine de Vaucluse, these names do not exclude us but resonate in a magical way – and even those who know the Vaucluse well must recognise that the poet has transformed a specific, physical geography into a universal, mythic geography. Char's sense of place is both acute and emotional: the topography of this land can be verified and has an intense physical presence but, more importantly, it is a world traversed by the enigmatic *Transparents* or *Clear-seeing Ones* who remind us of a time when our relationship with Nature was intimate, a world inhabited by the *Matinaux* or *Dawn Breakers* who live in and between night and day. Like Michaux's poetry, Char's work has an extraordinary visual force, an 'evidence'. But whereas Michaux creates imaginary countries in order to comment on the nature of reality, Char chooses to present his native region in order to reveal the truth that lies within reality.

Throughout his life, from his lonely childhood days until his last years when he chose to lead a secluded life near his birth-place L'Isle-sur-Sorgue and far from the literary and political feudings of Paris, Char found his inspiration in his long walks through the Vaucluse countryside and in his quiet, questioning observation of plants, animals, birds, rivers and meteorological changes. Many of his finest poems result from his determination to see fully in order to understand, to see in solitude in order to offer others the possibility of finding their own vision: for him, seeing authentically is a necessary first step towards the establishment of a sense of what I shall for the moment call 'being-in-the-world'.

However, in Char's poetry Nature is not a mere pretext for some late-come Romantic poetry. When Char looks at flowers, he uses his vision in a different way than did Wordsworth coming upon his 'crowd or host of golden daffodils'. When he writes of the river Sorgue which rises at the Fontaine de Vaucluse and runs through his home town, he is not imitating Petrarch who, fascinated by the isolated and enclosed Fontaine de Vaucluse, composed there many of his poems on Laura. Nor is he following Lamartine who gazed in narcissistic melancholy on his celebrated lake. The natural world around him provides no excuse for projection of his own moods and anxieties or for pathetic fallacy. Rather, he seeks to see fully, to *receive* the natural world and thence to discover oneness in difference always maintained as difference.

The focusing on individual objects is a feature of much modern French poetry. Yves Bonnefoy, for example, repeatedly portrays a salamander in order to meditate on presence and absence, and Francis Ponge writes sequences of poems on a pebble or a block of soap in order to offer a post-Cubist image of their quiddity or "thingness". Char's procedure is somewhat different – he seeks to show that no single object, be it animate or inanimate, can or should be perceived and interpreted in isolation but must be recognised as part of some vaster plan. For instance, in 'Complainte du lézard amoureux'/'Lament of a lovesick lizard' in *Les Matinaux/The Dawn Breakers*, the lizard is presented as a commentator, as a mediator who 'sees everything from his low wall' and can therefore 'tell the secrets of the earth'. For Char it is essential that we realise that all things, all beings have an autonomous existence and also function as revelatory *images*. His readers may well live in an environment in which there are no lizards or vipers, no crickets or cicadas, no Mistral winds, no high jagged mountains, no saxifrage or lavender, but the images hit home because they are offered as examples, as *paradigms*. Char should not be seen as a regional poet, but as a poet-thinker who universalises what he knows and sees personally, as a 'tragic optimist' who seeks to remind us that the past is always with and within us. In *La parole en archipel/ The Word as Archipelago* (1962), there is a sequence of four poems inspired by the prehistoric Lascaux cave-paintings. Each text refers us to an individual painting, yet the poetic act consists not in giving a verbal equivalent but in offering an interpretation of past images that we need to think about if we are to avoid simply admiring them as tourists. When writing of the painting of a young horse, Char marries his memory of this one image to references to African cults of the White Woman (a goddess of maternity) and to Georges de la Tour's paintings of Mary Magdalene (a symbol of repentance, death – and hope). The Lascaux painting is evoked but, more importantly, it is made the site of interpretation and appropriation. And the past, like the specific location of the Vaucluse, is shown to be both specific in its otherness or distance and universal in its present emotional and metaphysical value for us.

All of Char's poems articulate the experiences of a man confronting the physical world in a state of heightened emotion, be it as a lover, as a Resistance fighter, as a walker through the Provence landscape, as a 'Green' militant against nuclear power stations and the industrial polluting of rivers, as a spectator of paintings or as a reader of past writings. In many ways Char's poetic position is very close to that of the Thirties poet and critic Christopher Caudwell who stated that 'poetry is an adaptation to external reality. It is an emotional attitude to the world'. All Char's poems are highly personal (in *Fureur et mystère/ Furor and Mystery*, 1948, he affirms that 'The poem is always married to someone'), but they never seek to impose a purely subjective truth. Rather, they use language and images to urge readers into a sense of wonderment at, and a questioning of, the essence of existence.

Char's work should not, however, be seen as ontological or metaphysical in the sense that only scholars or philosophers can understand it. He himself said in an interview in 1948: 'I have my own personal critic. He's a poacher. When I've written something, I read it to him, and I can't help but laugh when people say that I'm hermetic, because he immediately understands, and says "Yes, you've got that right" or "You should change that word, and this one".' Another revelatory anecdote relates to Char's work in the Resistance. An officer sent from de Gaulle's headquarters in Algiers found it difficult to follow the imagistic language of Char's men. The poet explained that while slang is merely picturesque, the language shared by the Provençal Resistance fighters was metaphorical because of their intimate, direct contact with Nature, and he added that he used images in his dealings with them because 'when an image once strikes home, it is never ever forgotten'.

Char's poetry is extraordinarily visual even, as I say, for those who have never climbed the Provençal mountains or walked along the River Sorgue, but it also testifies to an almost mystical belief in the power of language. Words are our companions, our supports and our adversaries as we live out our lives, so we must be careful with them: as Char said in 1968, 'My love of words is so great that I cannot bear to squander them.' Char's poems are characterised by crispness and tension, but the individual terms employed are neither crisp nor fixed: each poem is like a limpid pool into which words have been dropped like pebbles, radiating out circles of connotations which never come completely to rest: in this poetry, words do not have single denotational meanings nor even "mere" ambiguity; they have etymological and connotational resonances and ultimately function as *echoes* of the lost language of a violent harmony.

For Char, poetry should not be categorical or didactic; it should lead readers to a state of lucidity in which they can perceive for themselves the meaning of the contradictions which fill and define the world. Yet no poet has full control over organised language and even less over individual words – which will always mean something different to different readers each of whom brings to their readings a personal (and often anxious) response to terms such as 'father', 'mother', 'love', and 'home'. Char is aware of this phenomenon, which, in a sense, is at the heart of his poetic project.

In his first collection *Les cloches sur le cœur/Bells on the heart* (1928), he used an imagery reminiscent of that of earlier French poets such as Laforgue and Apollinaire, an urban imagery of taxis, show-girls and electricity, but he later repudiated this volume and bought up and destroyed most of the 153 copies. While more than 50 years later the poet was to incorporate and rewrite fragments from this volume in some of his last works, this act of self-censorship, of what one might call poetic self-mutilation, is important for an understanding of Char's development. As he himself recognised, this volume is the work of a poet who is in search of his own voice – and who has not yet liberated himself from the influence of near-contemporaries or from the demands of formal poetic structures. Furthermore many of the texts are haunted, even scarred by his anguish at the deaths of his father and grandmother. They speak of a very private universe, of a childhood that could not be properly incorporated into his poetry until he had exorcised the ghosts and found a voice which was both individual and universal. Hence the repudiation of the volume.

The poems in *Les cloches sur le cœur/ Bells on the heart* were written between 1922 and 1926, the year in which Paul Éluard published *Capitale de la douleur/ Capital of suffering*. Char's discovery of this volume was to be decisive for his poetic career. He found there a contemporary voice which married the personal and the universal, the simple and the complicated, violence and harmony, love and disappointment (even anger). It was a book that ceased to look to the past for models and inspired Char to explore new ways of writing. In 1929 and at his own expense he published *Arsenal/ Arsenal*, a collection which heralds the true Charrian voice. Here there is much violence but most of the images are now drawn from Nature and the poet has discovered the complex virtue of simplicity, as in this poem:

L'amour
Être
Le premier venu

Love
Being
The first to come along

Char sent a copy of *Arsenal* to Éluard who immediately went to L'Isle-sur-Sorgue to meet the young poet and to invite him to Paris to meet other Surrealists such as Breton and Aragon. Char consequently joined the Surrealist group at the same time as Dalí and Buñuel and in 1930 published *Ralentir travaux/ Slow down men at work*, a text written collectively with Éluard and Breton. For the next five years he was an important member of the group, co-signing many tracts and open letters. More importantly, he began to read such major Surrealist precursors as Rimbaud, Lautréamont, the pre-Socratic philosophers and the great alchemists. He also engaged actively, and occasionally belligerently – with his fists – in their political battles. These were times of friendship (notably with Éluard, a surrogate elder brother), times of reading and self-examination, but Char was already more concerned with poetry as a way of dealing with the world than with Parisian and international quarrels about details of political ideology. During his membership of the Surrealist group, he above all explored different ways of being free, yet he could never fully accept that the unconscious should be privileged over the conscious, as the Surrealists as a whole did. The most important lesson that Char learned from Surrealism was that poetry can and must violate the comfortable rules of society and syntax. A consequence of this is that aggression can be poeticised in such a way that neither subject nor object is destroyed. Both are maintained in a state of creative, prospective suffering. Formal logic has no place in this thinking; what is privileged is *lived* experience and an often aggressive engagement with the Other, by which I mean anything outside of himself. While Char is primordially committed to writing about the Other, his poems testify to an aggression toward the object, be it an image or a poem he has created, a woman he loves, the reader, the text, language generally – or even himself. His poetry is profoundly sadomasochistic in its play with aggression and passivity. But he seeks not to destroy either subject or object but to maintain both in a state of suffering and heightened awareness. Char's exploration and presentation of the subject-object relationship as an interaction, as a *dialogue*, distinguishes him from the other Surrealists whose work is often generated by narcissism, by an obsessive need to define and describe everything in terms of their own fantasies and political positions. Char rejects this (willed) identification of subject and object which characterises most Surrealist poetry, especially that of André Breton, preferring to articulate his own sense of aggression in order to establish a new sense of (warring) harmony. Even in his love poems where he inevitably speaks of himself, we find an *expansive* rather than a *retracted* narcissism, that is to say he expresses his own deeply personal emotions in order to engage fully with some absolutely *other* – who is always both the beloved and the unknown reader.

Much later, in *À une sérénité crispée/ Towards a tense serenity* (1952), he explicitly confronted the problem of narcissism, writing: 'You should have drunk of the water, Narcissus, and not looked at yourself'. Narcissus, as mythic figure and as psychic structure, is finally perceived as culpable. By preferring his self-image to the nourishing and ever-changing transparency of the water, he has risked more than narcissistic imprisonment: he has denied freedom and even immortality both to the self and to the Other. In his love poem 'Lettera amorosa' (1953, definitive version 1964), Char most fully reveals how he has learned to incorporate images of violence and fantasies of death and resurrection into a tender but brutally honest text. This long poem warns against the dual temptations of idealisation and aggressiveness and proposes that reflection must be more than a narcissistic gazing at the self: we must both see our uniqueness and allow the world and other people to become part of ourselves and of our self-images.

All of Char's later poetry bears the traces of his contact with the Surrealist group, notably in his creation of juxtapositional images, but even during his period of allegiance to Surrealism he was seeking to write with moral seriousness and with simplicity (he rarely indulged in the linguistic firework-displays dear to Breton, Desnos and Queneau). Furthermore he always insisted on the creative control of the conscious: all of his poetry is firmly tied to the world and communicates a commitment to lucidity as the touchstone of existence. This is what led to his official break with the movement in December 1935 when he wrote in a public letter that 'Surrealism has committed itself to a course which is bound to lead it to the Retirement Home for Belles-Lettres and Violence'. Angry, cruel words – generated by his disappointment with colleagues who had in his view betrayed the ideal of fraternity and poetry. Although Char was reluctant to speak about his Surrealist period, whenever he did he would express his irritation with those who 'did in fact rather bore me'. But at the same time he would also insist on the importance of the lessons he had learned and especially the life-long friendships he had formed, notably with Éluard, Braque and Picasso.

In 1936, history – both social and personal – coincided with a literature of violence when the Spanish Civil War broke out and the poet contracted an acute case of septicaemia which almost led to his death. His rage against the senseless killing of children led to *Placard pour un chemin des écoliers/ Sign towards the long way round* (1937) in which he re-enacts his own childhood, now perceived in the context both of the Spanish child-victims and of his narrow escape from death. Yet already here we find his refusal to write poems which are too closely tied to individual events: for Char, if we are to be fully human, we must constantly engage in acts of resistance but we must also look beyond the specific aspects of individual events and atrocities in order to perceive their universality. Only then can we realise that oppression is always with us. In 1952 he wrote, 'Our most insidious enemy is what is happening today', by which he means that the defeat of a Hitler, a Franco or a Saddam Hussein is never enough: there will always be other – less obvious – oppressors, such as the State, the Church, even the education system. So, he insists, we must never at any moment allow ourselves to relax into thinking that human liberty has been assured once and for all.

The 1930s were a crucial decade in Char's moral, political and poetic development. He rejected Surrealism and what he called its 'clever but artificial' obsession with alchemy and Rimbaud's notion of verbal alchemy (which for some Surrealists merely meant language-games). He came close to death and was outraged by the atrocities committed during the Spanish Civil War. Later, he made a personal discovery of the horror of the Nazi persecution of Jews and 'communists': his first wife, Georgette Goldstein, was a Jewess and he was officially declared to be a Communist in 1941. These various factors lead him to join the Resistance forces and, known as 'le capitaine Alexandre', he initially masterminded sabotage attacks on the occupying Italian army and against the Nazis and then took charge of the SAP (Section Atterrissage Parachutage/landing-parachuting organisation) in Southern France. During his struggle against the occupying forces, he continued to write, although he did not show to his comrades his brief, passionate notes – which he agreed to publish only after the war. These *Feuillets d'Hypnos/Leaves of Hypnos* (1946) are a precious historical, moral as well as poetic document. They say much about how Resistance activity aided men to find themselves, about how deaths can be witnessed impotently, from a distance, and yet ultimately be perceived as a means of understanding life and what it should be. Many of these texts blaze with rage, especially when Char talks of intimate friends who were executed or sent to concentration camps and when he writes of his angry refusal of any and every tyranny. Yet scattered throughout these 237 notes are many highly moral, self-controlling, almost religious exhortations to go beyond rage, fury and hatred in order to continue effectively the struggle against oppression and to prepare for the future creation of a better world. In this respect, it is important to note that after the Liberation Char spent much time helping to establish dossiers which proved that his Resistance comrades had been true 'maquisards', but that he refused to participate in the shameful witch-hunt of alleged collaborators which he considered to be nothing more than 'a copy of what our enemy did when it was in power'. 'We must triumph over our rage and our disgust...' he wrote, 'in order to make both our actions and our morality nobler and more far-reaching.'

However, the demands of warfare and leading a Resistance group led Char to make difficult decisions which were to haunt him for the rest of his life. In 1946, he wrote a darkly mysterious poem 'L'extravagant'/'The act of madness', published in *Le poème pulvérisé/The pulverised poem* (1947), which ends with the statement that 'Spring does not exist'. Of all his texts, this was the one which for years he refused to discuss. 'You are forbidden to touch this poem – it's mine and mine alone,' he stormed at one critic and friend when pressed for an explanation. This refusal is a surprise when one remembers the poet's usual insistence that no text 'belongs' to its author once it is published. But in this case his reasons were understandable in that the poem does not speak of an extravagant or mad person but of an excessive *act*. In 1983 he finally explained to Paul Veyne that 'L'extravagant'/'The act of madness' was born out of his anguished decision to execute two young traitors, one of whom had betrayed forty-five of his comrades to the Gestapo who then shot them; the other was a dangerous collaborator. While Char has said that individual lives cannot have the same value in wartime as they do in peacetime, he was haunted by these executions, especially in the immediate post-war years when he was nauseated by the way in which both the Right and the Left in France were exploiting the Liberation. The actual poem makes no explicit reference to the executions, but this very silence is revelatory: it reminds us that poetry must always be about transformation – whatever details we may glean of its genesis, the text itself should remain as a trace of lived experience and, more importantly, as a metamorphosis of that experience.

Through his contact with the Surrealists, Char had discovered the communicational possibilities of a language which bypassed the rational, the conscious, the socially-determined; his experiences in the Resistance, when revolt had to be expressed in deeds rather than in words, taught him to beware of the temptation of merely playing with language. In his war notebooks he repeatedly articulates his awareness that words – and even poetry – become marginal when events demand active commitment, yet he also could not but continue to write, in secret, when not engaged in Resistance work. As he says in a revelatory note: 'I write briefly. I cannot *be absent* for any length of time. Saying all I wanted to say would become obsessive. The adoration of the shepherds no longer makes any sense for our planet.' By this he means that we cannot today permit ourselves either to indulge in self-centred expression or to be naïve, passive worshippers at any shrine: we need to be aggressive and even violent. So the problem of the place of poetry in the modern world was posed for him in a much more urgent way than for Hölderlin or even for Heidegger. In moments of danger, actions must take precedence over words, he recognises – but only words can both maintain and interrogate the memory of these events in and for future years.

All of Char's later work is shaped by his war-time experiences with language and silence, but it is also marked and enriched by an event which gave an anxious reality to the Surrealists' mystical, utopian view of language as magical. During his Resistance activity the code-word for one of the parachute drops was 'La bibliothèque est en feu' (The library is on fire). One of the containers exploded and set fire to the forest, illuminating the horizon, with the result that Char's group only just escaped with the other containers before the Gestapo arrived. Char's reaction was immediate: he contacted London to demand that the code be changed because 'I believe in the magic and in the authority of words' – since paper is made from wood, the code fatally determined that the forest should burn. Whatever we may individually wonder about such beliefs in the prophetic power of language, it is certain that Char was convinced that words can have a direct effect on the material world. This conviction can be traced back beyond his Surrealist period to the folklore of his childhood. For instance, he was familiar with the Provençal custom of setting out a glass of water in order to placate the 'returning spirits' and stated that he believed in ghosts even though he had never actually seen one. In both his Surrealist and his post-war periods, he wrote texts which tell of encounters which appear to be supernatural. This belief in a world beyond the physically verifiable links Char to pre-Christian thinking. His opposition to all religions that name their gods arose out of a deep mistrust of organised Christianity yet he nonetheless always retained a sense of the real possibility of transcendence. He might insist that 'It is fatal to abolish distance. The gods die only when they live amongst us'; yet his work is haunted by references to Christian figures and to Provençal and Classical mythologies. The latter may be familiar but for many readers the Provençal allusions are problematic.

One example from *Les Matinaux* is the use of *calendes* in 'Fête des arbres et du chasseur'/'Celebration of the trees and the hunter'. For many years I assumed that this referred to the Calends, the first day of any month in the Roman calendar and consequently I had problems understanding the full significance of the verse. French dictionaries and encyclopaedias were of no help, and none of the French writers I consulted could shed any light: I was left puzzling over why Char had used the term. Then, purely by chance, when chatting one day with a friend in Avignon, I discovered that in Provençal *calendes* means New Year (and in popular folklore is associated with the return of the dead). The meaning of the verse was suddenly clear, but this discovery was more than just a problem solved. It helped me to understand that when Char uses unfamiliar or archaic words, he does not intend to confuse or deter his readers. Rather he is reminding us that words mean different things in different contexts and that they often have a hidden history. Convinced that we increasingly need today to learn from the past which is all too swiftly disappearing from our ken, Char offers us enigmas to solve – in order to oblige us to construct a new and personal sense of presence.

Childhood: Solitude and Anger

The Child is father of the Man
WORDSWORTH

Touch me with noble anger
SHAKESPEARE (*KING LEAR*)

The child as a figure of innocence and wonderment haunts much European literature and is often associated with the notion of the privileged moment – when we both feel intensely and see harmony in the world. In the 'La chambre double'/'The Double room', Baudelaire defines this dual quality of consciousness as having 'the sufficient clarity and the delightful obscurity of harmony'. The creative tension described by Baudelaire is close to that proposed by the pre-Socratic philosophers Heraclitus, Empedocles and Parmenides whom Char admires above all other philosophers, notably for their insistence that true consciousness is about emotion as much as about rational perception. We have all had experiences when the object or scene at which we are gazing seems to separate itself from the daily flow of impressions and becomes intensely clear and important for us. However, these epiphanies or moments of illumination become increasingly rare as we grow older and our lives are dominated by professional concerns. While the Romantic poets may look back nostalgically at childhood, Char's attitude is essentially forward-looking: for him the past and the present exist in a relationship of complementarity and supplementarity which necessarily includes a straining towards the future. His vision of childhood is also very different from that of Proust who sees and uses the world of his childhood as *non-moi* (not me). For Char, the child 'sees the man in a simplified light. Therein lies the secret of their inseparability'.

In the privileged moment, the normal subject-object relationship is suspended, as is sequential, "horizontal" time or time-assuccession – and Char constantly insists on the importance of "vertical" time, of moments when we are removed from banal reality and experience the world intensely. His favourite image for this is the lightning flash which is both ephemeral and 'long', an illumination which lasts. The problem of reality is at the heart of his thinking, and his poetry seeks to merge the mystical impulses of childhood with the rational perceptions of adulthood and modern science. Yet always one senses that for Char these epiphanies are experienced in a state of isolation. Valéry uses the term *absence*, by which he means that the gazing person falls out of a world made of *signs* or abstract concepts into one made of *significances*. Rilke chooses to speak about *aloneness*, by which he means that in moments of heightened awareness we are cut off from the everyday world and become one with the cosmos. It is through childhood that we are raised above the banality of existence and are, as Rilke says, 'a place where heart and star are mingled', but while both Valéry's and Rilke's terms have a positive sense, Char, who shares their belief in epiphanies, sees absence and aloneness as also having a negative, destructive quality.

Char's thinking is certainly inscribed in this tradition which insists on the privileged moment and which associates the child with vision and imagination. He speaks, for instance, of imagination as 'my child' and repeatedly affirms that imagination distances itself from everyday reality in order to discover the real – which he defines in terms borrowed from Christianity as 'being not made' (*le réel incréé*). However, while the child is an important cultural concept which Char shares with many other writers, his own early lived experiences are the foundation of most of the major themes and indeed techniques of his work.

The youngest of four children, Char was a silent, lonely, sad and often angry boy who found solace in the companionship of the fisherfolk of L'Isle and in his long walks by the River Sorgue during which he had the double sense of being part of Nature and somehow separated from it. For instance, he once wrote that 'The hawthorn in flower was my first alphabet'. This is a testament to how a child learns experientially by seeing, touching and smelling rather than through school-lessons where language and logic supplant pure images. Yet the hawthorn also plays an important role in both Provençal folklore and Christian iconography: it cannot therefore be just a tree seen by a child on a walk but must function in his mind as a reminder that others have *already* interpreted it for him. For this reason it is important to know that his first memory was, at the age of three or four, that of the beauty of women – the beauty of his adored eldest sister Julia (who would much later tragically go mad) and that of his Italian nanny. This initial discovery of feminine beauty was decisive, but it brought with it another crucial discovery: everything that is not beautiful (and for him this means most of the world) is disastrous and destructive – many of his most passionate attacks on Nazism are articulated in terms of its ugliness. In other words, beauty is a moral force, a unifying principle which we must constantly seek to re-establish. He closes his war journal thus: 'In the darkness in which we live, there is not one single place for Beauty. Beauty must be everywhere.' Yet beauty reveals itself all too rarely and only in privileged moments, so one must struggle to rediscover and recreate it.

The discovery of beauty (and of its all too frequent absence) was soon followed by his experience of death. The first and most traumatic death was that of his father, the second that of his grandmother. In an interview in 1965, he said: 'When I was a child, death was my cousin. I lost my father in my eleventh year, then my maternal grandmother – the two people who loved and understood me best, and then some others.' His father's death led to financial problems for the family and to the exacerbation of his already difficult relationship with his mother who was 'always good to me, although often clumsy' but who felt that he had to be kept under firm control because he 'was never like other children'. More significantly, though, it left Char with a feeling of the injustice of life and death (his father represented 'equilibrium and justice' for him), and throughout his adult life he would fight against the injustice shown by individuals, by political ideologies and by all institutions of the State.

His elder brother 'persecuted' him from an early age and, when he was ten years old, he was so driven by his feeling of injustice that he persuaded Jean-Pancrace Nouguier, one of his L'Isle-sur-Sorgue mentors, to lend him a pistol so that he could kill him. Nouguier wisely refused to give him any bullets, so over the next few years Char hardened his fists by punching trees until he could finally knock his brother down (his brother's bullying is the key to 'L'adolescent souffleté'/'The slapped adolescent' in *Les Matinaux*). This episode is more than just a familiar story of sibling rivalry: it reveals how from an early age Char was convinced of the necessity to hit back, to combat injustice with violence. The importance of the loss of his father cannot be over-estimated, for it alerted Char to the anguished fact that life is rarely fair and that we are all condemned to confinement unless we rebel. In his 1928 poem 'Présence chère qui n'est plus'/'Dear presence no longer present', he writes:

L'essoufflement d'une vipère
Juste au-dessous de ce hallier
Fait toutes les tiges vibrer
Et moi j'appelle en vain mon père

The breathlessness of a viper
Here under the bushes hiding
Makes the stems rustle, makes them sing
And I call in vain for my father

The viper, that 'prince of misinterpretation' which snakes its way through much of Char's poetry and with which he identifies, is a crucial symbol, in that it emerges, breathlessly, from the dark depths of the earth, a fragile phallus which can punish with poison when attacked, a creature associated with death and life – but a natural creature which we should not judge out of fear. It frightens many people, yet only because it is different, because we don't understand its natural laws. Char was unlike other children and frightened his mother because she couldn't understand or accept his otherness. Her response took the form of an attempt to control and socialise him – and this he never forgave her, just as he never forgave her imposition of sexual repression. This explains his aggressive sexualisation of mothers in his poetry and in some part his life-long delight in and need of women who would offer another image of Woman.

The death of his father had one further effect. His mother was afraid of death and corpses, so the boy Char kept a vigil over both his father and grandmother, watching and tending the fire in his dying father's room and shocking his mother when she found him in bed holding his dead grandmother ('it was the greatest proof of my love for her'). In an interview in 1977, he said that his principal memory of his father's illness was 'the battle of the burning logs'. The awful inevitability of death and the sorrow and impotent anger of the watching son are powerfully present here, as in Dylan Thomas 'Do not go gentle into that dark night'. But one image from Char's harrowing experience was made creative – years later he described how poetry came to him: 'like a bird's feather settling on my window. And then suddenly, the fireplace became the battleground of burning logs – and the battle has not yet ended'. Fire as consumption and warmth, sound and silence, violence and harmony, death and resurrection: these are some of the poles around which Char's poetry is thought.

Another family death haunted Char and contributed both to his dislike of his mother and to his fascination with women: that of Julia Rouget, his father's first wife who died of tuberculosis in 1886 after only one year of marriage. In the marvellously harmonious, melodious and for once nostalgic poem 'Jacquemard et Julia'/ 'Jacquemard and Julia' in *Le poème pulvérisé/The pulverised poem* (1947), Char hymns the love his father lost, the love he himself was to seek all his life, the love which like Beauty seems destined always to be absent. Two years after Julia's death, Char's father married her sister Marie-Thérèse, but the poet never really forgave his mother for taking the place of the aunt he knew only through his father's stories and his own fantasies. Perhaps he loved Julia because she was loved briefly but intensely – but also because she never became a mother. In his only dream-recital 'Eaux-mères'/ 'Maternal waters' (1932), the mother-figures of 'my mother' and 'my sister, mother of my nephew' are repudiated and the dream-narrator appropriates for himself maternal love for the drowned child he resuscitates. One of Char's most committedly Surrealist texts, it is based on a real dream to which he added only a few "waking" commentaries. As such it is biographically and psycho-analytically illuminating, in that it reveals both the force of the poet's angry rejection of biological mothers and his need to exert some conscious control over his fantasies.

Both at home and at school (which he loathed and repeatedly presents as a repressive force), Char was silent, but this silence was not a mere refusal to conform. It was a *waiting*, a listening to Nature until he found the words and, more importantly, the voice he needed to express his sense of what Heidegger calls Dasein or being-in-the-world, *indwelling*. Born of childhood solitude, this silence led the adult poet to a meditation on the adequacy and exactitude of language and his writings are all marked by a sparing use of adjectives. For him, the *thing* (animal, plant or whatever) is best evoked by a bare noun which in its very nudity calls the reader into an activity both of remembering and of creating. This is why he sees childhood vision as 'a marvellous miracle' – because children 'remain children and see through our eyes'. For Char, as for Wordsworth, the Child is indeed the father of the Man, above all because his innocence is indestructible: childhood is always about progress, adulthood is all too often about defeat.

This explains why in March 1937 he hesitatingly, apologetically, dedicated the volume *Placard pour un chemin des écoliers/Sign towards the long way round* to the children of Spain who would never know the beauty and wonder of the natural world. When he rages against the 'butchers' who are filling communal graves with 'the throbbing bodies of children', he is fulminating not only against all political oppression but against the injustice and stupidity of a world which denies itself the possibility of illumination and growth through the vision of children.

Although Char was a solitary child who seems to have had no close school-friends, he did have several mentors who rehabilitated his childhood and adolescence, the most important being Louis Curel, a farm worker whose nobility he praises in 'Louis Curel de la Sorgue'/'Louis Curel of the Sorgue' (in *Fureur et Mystère/Furor and Mystery*). In a 1977 interview, Char described both Curel and Jean-Pancrace Nouguier as 'Marcus Aurelius figures for me', but Curel clearly also took over the role of the dead father. For Char, he was a model of probity, a sort of Stoic hero who through his intimate union with Nature discovered and was able to reveal the beauty and harmony inherent in existence. The reference to Marcus Aurelius is significant, for Char is evidently thinking not only about Stoicism as fixity and resistance but about the serenity of acceptance which Marcus Aurelius advocates: 'All that is in tune with thee, O Universe, is in tune with me'; 'Meditate often on the intimate union and mutual interdependence of all things in the Universe'.

In Char's view, poetry, like life, must simultaneously involve a passionate and a meditative relationship with the world. This combination leads to the stance of moral, heroic resistance which is Char's ideal response to the disappointments and tragedies of existence. 'Louis Curel de la Sorgue'/'Louis Curel of the Sorgue' ends thus: 'There is at this time a man who is standing upright, a man in a field of rye, a field like a machine-gunned choir, a field which is saved.' Here we have the essence of Char's morality: we must stand, unbowed but also attentive, in the midst of disaster and destruction in order to be *witnesses* and ultimately secular saviours – who will make constructive sense of the *bêtise* of destructiveness. As his friend Georges Braque states: 'Fatalism is not, as generally supposed, a passive state'.

Louis Curel's essence is defined by his belonging to, and involvement with, his surroundings which are no simple background: they are alive, symbolic, part of him and different from him. They speak to him and reveal him to himself more even than they reveal themselves to him. Indeed, throughout all Char's work the natural world is the crucial interlocutor, even in the love poems. Octavio Paz, whose thinking is very close to Char's, writes in an essay on the prose fiction of D.H. Lawrence and Malcolm Lowry: 'A landscape never refers only to itself; it always points to something else, to something beyond itself. It is a metaphysic, a religion, an ideal of man and the cosmos' (*Alternating Current*).

If the natural world is the primal and primary interlocutor, it is always perceived and presented as multiple. In 'Divergence', for example, the narrow-headed horse is posited as the enemy of the 'lazy-heeled poet'. This horse pulling the plough that 'wounds' the earth is the servant of the farmer who has to work according to the irregular imperatives of the weather; it is both a symbol of loyalty and a reproach for inactivity. In Char's work, the image or symbol is never monovalent, and the plodding plough-pulling horse of 'Divergence' is just one incarnation of the animal which represents liberty, fertility and rebellion in other poems: the natural world cannot be neatly codified but will always be and mean more than any single interpretation can say.

In Char's poetry, there is often an apparent identification with creatures, as in 'Complainte du lézard amoureux'/'Lament of the love-sick lizard' and 'Jouvence des Névons'/'Youth at *Les Névons*' in *Les Matinaux*. The identification is desired, even willed, but there is always a sense of the otherness of the creatures, and the poems articulate something more than empathy. Like Rilke, Char benefited from strange kinds of inspiration generated by his close observation and contemplation of animals. Rilke speaks of the marvel of being able 'to see into a dog as you pass, to see into it... to get inside it, to its exact centre, the point where it starts being a dog'. For Rilke, this leads to a feeling of intense joy, to a moment which is blissful (*selig*), precisely because it demands the total sur-render of self-consciousness, to a kind of anonymity. Valéry thinks in similar terms. Standing on London Bridge, he says 'I am what I am, I am what I see'. Char spoke several times with me about Valéry's vision of a creatively narcissistic mode of consciousness, but he insisted that his own ambition was somewhat different. He sought what Rilke calls *Einsehen* (seeing-into), yet he was always aware that, as Heidegger points out, when we say 'the same' we necessarily think 'difference' and vice versa. This is why the natural world is so important for him. It is the main source of our know-ledge about ourselves, yet we are all too often separated from it, especially in the modern technological world. Consequently we lose touch with the so-called "primitive" beliefs, superstitions and religions which have shaped and given form to our indwelling.

Char's project is therefore paradoxical: he wants to present, but he must also project and receive. In this, his poetry is substantially different from that of Ponge, who seeks to remind us of the inadequacy of descriptive language, and from that of Bonnefoy, whose repeated presentations of the salamander are structured by a concern with the binary opposition of presence and absence. Both Ponge and Bonnefoy are perhaps easier to read, but Char's complex, anxious meditations may be more resonant for those who take the time to read and re-read them and to discover light in their darkness, simplicity in their complexity.

A "difficult" poet, Char expects nothing more or less from his readers than an attention to what the world actually is – and is becoming. After all, if an untutored Provençal poacher can understand and even correct his texts, Char must be saying something we can all understand, whether or not we have read any other poetry or philosophy. Cultural tradition can of course be tyrannical and draw attention away from what is there on the page, as we seek, for instance, to impose a grid of Heraclitean or Heideggerian philosophy or Freudian thinking on Char's work. This is not to say that the traditions of European poetry and philosophy are unimportant for Char. Indeed the opposite is true, although he tends to focus on thinkers who were not yet canonised by the Academy when he was responding to their ideas. One thinks immediately of Heraclitus whom he read in the 1930s when only a few specialist scholars studied him, or of Sade who has only recently been "rescued" from the interdiction of the Vatican's Index and made available to book-buyers. His choice of precursors is dictated not by the demands and expectations of prevailing intellectual currents but by what these writers say and do to him. Rebellion? Perhaps. More accurately, a self-affirmation which refuses the notion that we must follow what others tell us to read, a conviction that we must find our own past in order to create our individual present.

If Nature plays a major symbolic and pedagogic role in Char's poetry, it is because children who reject social and familial authority have no other immediate and ever-present mentor – and don't we all live this rebellion? Don't we all need alternative authorities? Rebelling against all forms of institutionalised authority, we seek other parents, other schools, other determining myths and legends, other heroes and heroines, because at all points in our lives we need structures, or at least some form of structuring. Char's work constantly returns to this problem – and so reminds us of our own individual revolts against the dictates handed down from on high by our elders with no dialogic consultation. It also reminds us that we can learn what Nature is only by experiencing it directly. For instance, he frequently explained to me that night does not come from the sky but rises from the earth like an emanation, like a ground-mist, as soon as the sun has set. Once told, one realises that this is true, but it does go against traditional notions taught at home and at school.

The anguished concern with oppression and loss explains in some measure Char's fascination with the *Transparents*, the *Clear-seeing Ones* who lived and thought outside the parameters of "normal" society and with whom the boy Char spent much time, preferring to tell his mother that he had committed the 'crime' of going to the café rather than admitting to consorting with them, such was their ostracised position in bourgeois society. They were wanderers, but unlike the Romany gypsies they rarely roamed far from their Provence. They spoke a language whose strangeness revitalised dead metaphors and excavated dark memories, while also illuminating the present. They told of a world which, though not yet gone, was disappearing, of a world which believed in ancient gods and, more importantly, in ancient mysteries. Throughout his life Char was a fervent atheist and anti-Catholic: when writing of his vigil at the bedside of his dying grandmother in 'Intérieur'/'Interior' (1928) and again in a reworked version 'Le veilleur naïf'/'The naïve watcher' (1983), he ends both poems with almost exactly the same words: 'the dying woman suddenly became just a *thing*'. This refusal of Christian salvation and transcendence is, however, countered by a committed belief in the sacred as represented by Nature and by the forces of Strife and Love which, according to the pre-Socratics, structure the world as a cycle of becoming. Above all, Char clings to a sense of *belonging*, of being part of the world. Heidegger calls Hölderlin the poet of the Time Between (between the departure and the return of the gods). Char is a poet of this same temporal betwixtness. He repeatedly refers back to the lost past which has much to teach us, but he does this in order to propel us onwards into a new relationship with existence and the cosmos wherein we shall rediscover both innocence and wisdom – and we should note that for Char *discovery* is always more important than *invention* which is merely a paltry and materialistic defence against the wonderful mystery of indwelling.

The Relativity of Poetry

Full of merit, yet poetically
Man dwells on this earth
FRIEDRICH HÖLDERLIN

Merit in poets is as boring as merit in people
WALLACE STEVENS

All poetry is about a passionate, if sometimes despairing, relationship with the world. In Char's case, this relationship is one of anger as well as one of hope. If he often castigates humankind for its cowardice and lack of commitment to others, he also repeatedly uses images of growth (the chrysalis which will become a butterfly or the seed which will become a plant, the flower which will become a fruit). He loves his fellow-beings, without pity, without any illusions or delusions...and always determinedly. As I have said, he lives and writes in a state of 'tragic optimism', in a state where pessimism and optimism are not so much at war as succeeding each other in a cycle that moves him and us on towards the creation of a world which will finally recognise its inherent transcendence. Yet the poet is always writing for someone else, for the unknown reader. Therein lies his grandeur – and his solitude.

Traditionally the love poem is seen as the celebration of a relationship, whether this relationship be consummated or not, real or imaginary. In his love poems Char hymns sexual and emotional complicity ('L'amoureuse en secret'/'Loving him secretly' and 'Recours au ruisseau'/'Recourse to the river'), laments absence ('Le carreau'/'The window-pane'), warns against jealousy ('Corail'/ 'Coral'); he speaks of the necessity of sharing the experience of a fleeting love with others, be they friends or readers ('Anoukis et plus tard Jeanne'/'Anoukis and later Jeanne'); he challenges the narcissism which is at the heart of much loving and much poetry ('À la désespérade'/'At the Désespérade'). All this was lived by the poet; all this has much in common with the work of such major French love poets as Ronsard, Baudelaire and Éluard. However in Charrian love poetry the beloved is never the sole focus or pretext for his thinking and writing but is always part of his desire to understand and describe existence in its manifold differences. From his childhood discovery of the beautiful whiteness of his Italian nanny's breast until his death, Char loved and was loved by many women – indeed one of his friends has written that *la sua lista* was longer than Casanova's! Loved and loving women were essential to the poet's personal life and well-being, but in his writing they become poetic *figures* whose function is similar to that of animals, rivers, plants and trees: they remind the reader that all aspects of our lives are intertwined, that every relationship is ultimately about our indwelling.

While Char loved often and passionately, his poetic presentation of Woman is marked by a certain male chauvinism. *Le Visage nuptial*/*The Nuptial Countenance* (1938) ends thus: 'This is the sand dead, this the body saved:/Woman breathes, Man stands upright'. Like the field in 'Louis Curel de la Sorgue', the body is saved and the male lover is upright, while the female lover 'breathes', is horizontal and passive. There can be no doubt that Char considered women to be inferior, his sexism being as calm and assured as it was absolute. He saw himself as the liberator of all those he loved, giving them the freedom of poetry as well as the freedom of eroticism, and above all freeing them from the constraints of society's rules and expectations. When Char writes of love, it is always about desire which must *remain* desire and not slide into repetition, fidelity, marriage, and certainly not into parenthood: like Baudelaire and Sade, he cannot love woman's procreative potential, and indeed his conception of desire is an essentially male one. For him as for many of the Surrealists, encounters are best when fleeting – like a lightning-flash: therein lies their intensity and their permanence. 'The friend who stays,' he writes, 'is no better than the friend who leaves. Fidelity is a usurped territory.' There are echoes here of the parable of the Prodigal Son but above all a sense that sexual fidelity is irrelevant, whereas fidelity to moral principles is paramount.

'Anoukis et plus tard Jeanne'/'Anoukis and later Jeanne' is one of Char's most beautiful and resonant love poems and one of his most revelatory. A celebration of love, 'Anoukis' is traditional in that it sings the praises of a beloved whom the poet wants to share 'poetically' with others. It is typically Charrian in its insistence that love leads to a coincidence with Nature and with folklore. In Provençal mythology, Anoukis is both the goddess who watches over river-bends and a figure of destiny who kills her victims by embracing them. The poem's full force, however, can be realised only when one knows a little of its source. In conversations with Char, Paul Veyne discovered that Char did indeed have a chance with an Anoukis figure (Jeanne) and that he swiftly passed to a sexual relationship with her. More worryingly, Veyne gives some details of the end of this encounter. One of Char's painter friends saw her and made the following request: 'René, give her to me, I love her too much'. Char 'gave' her to him!

Poetic sharing is admirable; actual sharing of women by "giving" them to friends is problematic or, rather, shameful, in that it presupposes that men actually have proprietorial power over women and can dispose of them as they will. The anecdotal basis of the text is disturbing to anyone committed to sexual equality, and many of us will be shocked by the fact that Veyne has no information to offer about the woman's reactions. However, the poem itself articulates a transcendance of individual experiences. Anoukis is Jeanne, his best friend's sister, a goddess, his destiny, all women in one, an incarnation of women. She can be loved and hymned in a poem only because she can be, *has been*, discarded – and has been made into a figure, a symbol. All too often, Char's love poems, like those of Baudelaire, have been (mis-)interpreted as being for and about individual women, but a close attention to his work reveals that his first and last beloved is poetry – which transforms the anecdotal or biographical into the archetypal and the mythic. At the heart of his poetic, intellectual and erotic thinking lies his conviction that 'the poem is the consummation of a love which maintains desire as desire'.

Poetry, Beauty, Nature, love, desire, justice: these are the forces which structure Char's universe. And each of them involves violence. The poet experienced violence from the moment he could see and relate to the world: the emotional violence of his mother, the physical bullying of his elder brother, the necessary violence of the ploughman 'wounding' the earth, the regretful violence of the hunter who kills birds 'to keep the tree for himself', the natural violence of snakes, animals, birds and insects, of sun, storm and snow. The natural world is full of predators and preys whose warrings are necessary to the balance of nature. This Char discovered as a child who initially identified with the role of victim. However his reading of the pre-Socratic philosophers, notably Heraclitus and Empedocles, led him to recognise that conflict is a cosmic force and ultimately a moral force. Heraclitus declares that the universe consists of a struggle, that justice is a conflict and that all existence is determined by discord. He insists on the creativity which springs from a balanced strife between opposites. If conflict is natural and inevitable, Man/the poet must always respond by an act of resistance: 'I will never write a poem of acquiescence' (*Fureur et mystère/ Furor and Mystery*).

Char's angry revolt is directed outward at a world in which innocent children are killed, oppressors torture and tyrannise, and past traditions and beliefs are replaced by the selfishness of materialism. At times we must withdraw temporarily in order to find our strength, we must 'desert' as he urges in 'Conseil de la sentinelle'/'The Guard's advice', in other words, reject the entire system of oppression until we have rebuilt our ability to rebel. In this, there is no cowardice, rather a recognition that vulnerability is inherent in us all and that it can be creative and progressive only when it is allied to an active aggressivity.

The poet himself is both aggressor and aggressed – as is his poetry. And given the fact that his poetry is driven by an erotic desire for violent union with Woman, with Nature and with Poetry, we may go so far as to describe his poetry as sadomasochistic. Char's godmother Louise Roze was a descendant of the Marquis de Sade's lawyer and as an adolescent Char discovered in her library some autograph letters of the 'divine marquis' (or the 'violet man' as he calls him). This led him to read Sade's work and to discover not the social philosopher that many praise today, but a champion of erotic desire as violent, multiple and often self-contradictory who had an almost nihilistic conception of Nature as the victim of man's ferocity. While the Sadean obsession with orifices, real or created, finds no place in Char's writing, the presentation of eroticism as a reversible process of cruelty haunts several of his early poems. After his Surrealist period he abandoned much Sadean thinking, perceiving both harmony and the potential for rebirth in both love and Nature, but the concept of reversibility was to inform all of his mature work.

Like his Surrealist friends in the 1930s, he became fascinated by the work of Freud which offered a theoretical validation of the mobility both of his poetry and of his emotional and intellectual positions. For Char, the poet must assign himself an object which is both victim and 'dangerous'. This is why I describe his work as sadomasochistic – not because of any writing about sexual 'perversion' but because of the way in which it functions as poetry. For Freud, activity and passivity are universal characteristics of sexual life and the libido dictates all of our actions and decisions. If Char can exalt the love-making of praying mantises, in which the female bites off her partner's head at the moment of full consummation, he must see himself as the 'active' male and also as the 'passive' victim of erotic violence. However the Freudian active/passive opposition is used by the poet mainly as a theoretical model for a poetry in which meaning emerges from the tension which always exists in language as in life: in all of Char's work, there is a creative struggle between fraternal duty and individual desires, between the erotic and the moral, between the emotional and the intellectual, between the realistic and the metaphysical.

Violence and delicacy work together and against each other in his texts and slowly the poetic Word, the *logos*, reveals itself as an ardent force. For Char, the sun is a source of violence, burning, evaporating, killing; but, more importantly, it is a noble counter-aggression liberating the persecuted from the 'plague of false knowledge'. Since this 'false knowledge' is monovalent certainty, humans need liberation, not liberty. Like Gide and Sartre, albeit in a different way, Char believes that freedom is a *process,* never a fixed state won and retained once and forever.

Paradoxically perhaps, liberation comes from an active acceptance of difference rather than from a single conviction of what is right and just. In the universe described in *Les Matinaux/The Dawn Breakers*, birds illuminate our world and are killed, trees provide a warming shade and are set alight by the hunter's cartridge ('Fête des arbres et du chasseur'/'Celebration of the trees and the hunter'); dogs are faithful and tormented ('Les Transparents'/'The Clearseeing'); windows are openings and mirrors ('Le carreau'/'The window-pane'); mountains are hostile and generous, rivers hide and reveal, are sterile and productive, but their violence is always magical ('Cet amour à tous retiré'/'This love lost to all'). In an open letter to Georges Bataille in 1950, Char asserted that the modern world will never rediscover 'a relative harmony, its burning diversity' until the 'problem of incompatibilities' is seriously posed. Earlier in a brief essay on Heraclitus, he speaks of 'the exhilarating union of opposites' which is 'the indispensable creative foundation of harmony'. This abiding concern with opposites, with dialectics, although reinforced by his reading of Heraclitus, Sade, Hegel, Freud and Heidegger, has its roots in Char's childhood observations of the natural world.

Nowhere is this better seen than in 'Fête'/'Celebration', composed for four Catalan 'maquisards' or Resistance fighters who could not return to Spain after the Liberation of France. Stylistically simple so that these modern-day troubadours could easily remember and sing it, the poem presents a series of images that underline the warring contradictions of Nature, and – crucially – the figure of humankind. The 'melancholy hunter' inadvertently destroys the forest that he loves and that is the habitat of his prey. While the poem has often been interpreted as an indictment of human interference in Nature, 'Fête'/'Celebration' says and does something more: a characteristically Charrian allegory, it speaks as much of poetic creation as of the violence and the killing which mark so much animal and human behaviour. The hunter is melancholy not because he intends to kill in order 'to keep for himself the tree and its long-suffering gloom' but rather because he dares to take no truly decisive action and so release the creativity inherent in all existence. When he finally fires, his cartridge accidentally sets fire to the forest. Yet the blaze, though consuming, is above all illuminating. Like the gnomic utterances of the *Clear-seeing Ones*, this allegory refuses and challenges the rigidity of traditional allegory, offering a transcendence of received logic. Like Goethe's butterfly which dies and is transfigured in the candle-flame, Char's poetry transforms matter into blazing light and destroys the world in order to recreate it in a more beautiful form. Throughout his work we find this central image of the blaze, whether it be the fire in the father's room which suddenly blazes up and inspires him to write, the lightning-flash which is simultaneously ephemeral and eternal and lights up our darkness, the forest-fire which by illuminating defers death, or the burning of the harvested fields which ensures a new and stronger growth. In *À une sérénité crispée/ Towards a tense serenity*, he affirms: 'Beauty sets fire to everything in our sheaf of darkness which must be set alight'; in 'Note sibérienne'/'Siberian note' (*Aromates chasseurs/ Hunting herbs*, 1975), he asks: 'Why then this repetition: we are a spark of unknown origin and always set fire ahead. This fire, do we hear it wheeze and cry out at the very moment when we are consumed? Nothing, except that we were suffering, so much that in its centre the vast silence was splitting'; in *Le poème pulvérisé/ The pulverised poem*, he hymns the 'Nomadic spark which dies in its fire'. Life and death are not perceived as a simple cycle: while Char's imagery is drawn from Nature, he is never satisfied with the life-death-resurrection cycle that Western culture has installed as the most optimistic description of existence. If his poetry and thinking are radical, this is because he sees that existence is not – or at least should not always be – bound by the tyranny of Time. From the past, we must retain only moments of transcendance and transfiguration, recognising that the Christian tradition tells us that Christ's Transfiguration not only reveals his divinity but prefigures his mortal death. Memory is 'death's great ally', for it prevents us from looking onward performatively to moments when sequential time may be crossed by vertical, eternal time, when the world is ablaze with illumination. This is the form of harmony which Char finds, advocates and creates in his poetry, hence his insistence on such images as the plateau which is a *continuous* summit not a temporary high point or the lightning-flash which reveals the permanence of illumination in the split-second of its occurrence.

In 'La Sorgue'/'The Sorgue: a song for Yvonne' (from *La fontaine narrative/The narrative fountain* of 1947), he hymns the 'River where the lightning ends and my house rises/Rolling to the steps of oblivion the rubble of my reason'. Running from the Fontaine de Vaucluse and encircling L'Isle-sur-Sorgue on three sides, the Sorgue is both a reality and a mythic figure but above all it is a constant presence which reminds the poet that all things are multiple and that we must maintain a position of simultaneous revolt and fraternity. For centuries the Sorgue supported the entire town which lived from fishing but it was later punished by the industrial pollution of a paper-making factory; its waters are still astonishingly transparent but are now dangerous; it is a symbol of death and survival. The poem ends with an invocation to the Sorgue which resumes Char's moral attitude: 'Keep me violent and the friend of the bees on the horizon'.

Poetic language is the most challenging and disquieting of all languages, in that it both juxtaposes differing stances and self-consciously explores and proclaims its own silences, inadequacies, redundancies and possibilities. At the same time, it is always inscribing itself inescapably but voluntarily into a history of previous thinking. Modern French poetry is perhaps more explicitly intertextual than any since the Renaissance, in that the past is woven into the present with both gratitude and a certain aggression, as poets seek to delineate their own space. Char's implacable stance occasionally led him to attack poets who had in his view slipped into mere word-play. For him, poetry should be essential, that is to say, central to our lives rather than a marginal decoration. For this reason, he insists on repositioning poetry in contemporary culture by urging us to read differently and so to relearn the lessons of past moral thinkers. If there is one statement which illuminates Char's attitude to our shared heritage, it is his favourite fragment by Heraclitus which prefigures much of Heidegger's thinking on sameness and difference: 'You never step twice into the same river.' Each experience we have, be it of love, Nature or poetry, is always a repetition yet always an innovation.

Hölderlin's crucial question, brilliantly considered by Heidegger in his oracular 1946 lecture on Rilke, 'Wozu Dichter in dürftiger Zeit' (What are poets for in a destitute time?) is an anxious question that Char repeatedly poses both to himself and to his readers. Like Hölderlin, he thought of the poet as 'the priest of the invisible'; like Heidegger, he conceived of poetry as a renovation of experience and as the site of truth or, more accurately, of *aletheia* (unveiling or unconcealedness). However, while the sacred is ever-present in his work and while he too merits the appellation given by Heidegger to Hölderlin of the poet of the Time Between, Char's insistence on the value of poets and on our need for them has a political edge. Poets must unveil truth and in so doing must challenge all the systems of oppression which shape the world in which they live and write. The poet is someone who must have moral courage, integrity (and indeed ferocity) and must consequently judge. Yet this social merit must also be traversed by moments of illumination, by colourful play with the lexicon and with folklore. Char essentially agrees with Hölderlin's view of the difference between merit and poetry, but he is also close to Wallace Stevens' position, believing that authentic merit is not propriety but must be splashed through by vivid personal experiences. This is one reason why he so admires such artists as Picasso, Braque and Arpad Szenes, in that their paintings marry intellectuality to emotion, graphism to colour. Above all, poetry must use its potential to disquiet. As he says in the last statement of 'Rougeur des Matinaux'/'Redness of the Dawn Breakers': 'In short, if you do destroy, let it be with nuptial tools'.

Seamed through by references to past works and past thinking, Char's poetry demands a reading that includes but also goes beyond local, personal knowledge, a reading that accepts that we can understand fully only if we attend to what has been prepared for us. In 'Cet amour à tous retiré'/'This love lost to all' from *Les Matinaux* we find the following stanza:

> The violence was magical;
> A man sometimes died,
> But as death seized him,
> A trace of amber would seal his eyes.

Violence, death, magical transformation: these Charrian thematic constants are presented here, simply, in one stanza that poses no interpretative difficulty for the reader. Except...why the amber? Most of us vaguely recognise its ritual importance, yet Char's usage is calculated to activate its multiple cultural resonances. Since Thales in 600 B.C., we know that amber (*electron* in Greek) has magnetic properties – it absorbs excess electrical charges from the person rubbing it. The tears of amber shed by Apollo when expelled from

Mount Olympus symbolise his nostalgia for a lost paradise and the promise of Elysium. Prehistoric insects have been preserved (and made beautiful) in amber, hence the Egyptians' use of amber in their embalming processes. Both the Celts and Christians saw amber as a symbol of spirituality and sanctity. Like so many of the symbols that Char uses, amber is plurivalent and intercultural. This means that readers can never fix on one single meaning and will in each successive reading privilege one or other of the possible connotations. Such a dismantling of the notion of textual authority is characteristic of Char's work in that he both accepts that the reader is the co-creator of his poems and also wishes to push the reader into an exploration of his or her own responses to superficially simple texts which are in fact creatively unstable. Although Char disliked the term *aphorism*, preferring the neutral 'short text', his poetic utterances do have the contestatory force of pre-Socratic aphorisms in that they juxtapose the explicit and the implicit, continuity and discontinuity. His writings therefore demand that readers accept that they are both the victims and the operators of a 'nuptial' violence (and create problems for any translator!).

If Char's imagery is often taken from his native Provence, his thinking is far from Eurocentric, largely perhaps because of his encounters with France-based painters from other continents, such as Wilfredo Lam and Zao Wou-Ki. With someone as widely read as Char, it is always difficult to know exactly whom he had or had not read, but it is interesting that his poetics, like his philosophical thinking, is very similar to that of Octavio Paz, who wrote in *The Bow and the Lyre*:

> Poetic creation begins as violence to language. The first act in this operation is the uprooting of words. The poet wrests them from their habitual connections and occupations: separated from the formless world of speech, words become unique, as if they had just been born. The second action is the return of the word: the poem becomes an object of participation. Two opposing forces inhabit the poem: one of elevation or uprooting, which pulls the word from language; the other of gravity which makes it return. The poem is an original and unique creation, but it is also reading and recitation: participation. The poet creates it; the people, by recitation, re-create it. Poet and reader are two moments of a single reality. Alternating in a manner that may aptly be called cyclical, their rotation engenders the spark: poetry.

Char's poetry begins in violence – in his just anger at all betrayals of freedom and in his determination to release language from the straitjacket of conventional usage. It ends in the (never-ending) work of reading which necessarily recognises that the universe exists as multiple by virtue of division and oppositions.

The Complications of Simplicity

Art is the only thing that can go on
mattering once it has stopped hurting.
ELIZABETH BOWEN

Life may change, but it may fly not;
Hope may vanish, but can die not;
Truth be veiled, but still it burneth
Love repulsed, – but it returneth!
SHELLEY

If Char's relationship with himself and his subjects may be defined as sadomasochistic, the workings of his texts are no less violent, albeit in a different way. Thematically, his work is dominated by suffering, woundings, deaths, all of which are for him potentially creative, a source of transformatory radiance – as all farmers, fisherfolk and hunters intuitively know. A child of the Vaucluse countryside, Char realised this from an early age and wrote of what he saw. And he wrote as he saw, hence his definition of the poet as 'a man of simplicity'. However, his vision or *inseeing* is not, as I have suggested, that of modern urban, industrialised man; although his poacher friend could immediately grasp the meaning of his poems, most modern Europeans have lost the ability to see the world around them. So poetry must be more than a mirror of reality and must re-open our eyes.

The twentieth century is above all the age of the image, of the spectacle, yet the barrage of images which daily assails us has had the effect of blinding us to the fact that true seeing is an act of active engagement and interpretation rather than one of passive reception. When in 1938 Char sent to his friend Christian Zervos, the editor of *Cahiers d'art*, two poems he had composed on paintings by Courbet and Corot, he spoke in his covering letter of 'the complications of poetry...the simplicity of painting'. His thinking then, as throughout his life, was not determined by Platonic or Hegelian hierarchies but by a belief that language has a duty to be 'complicated' in order to lead us on toward a new vision – like that of Rimbaud who wished to reinvent language so that we could once more see authentically. His was no intellectual project, as was that of Valéry whose difficulty is a strategy to ensure concentration on the workings of his poetry – Char frequently proclaimed that he was not an intellectual but 'a man of desire'. Rather, his poetry works to remind us that language must speak again of our primal roots. But the poet can achieve this only be reminding us that language, though the prism through which we can (hope to) apprehend reality, is necessarily also the vehicle of centuries of cultural accretion; consequently the poet must work both with and against history. If Wordsworth can write of 'intimations of immortality', Char cannot but write of 'intimations of origin'. However, sentimental nostalgia must be resolutely refused and the origin must constantly be made present as the future towards which we strain: 'To live is to obliterate a memory', as Char said in an interview. The past is consequently not to be rewritten or recuperated in purely personal terms; it is to be discovered, new and different, as a 'shared presence'.

The project is idealistic, but it is also problematic in that even today reading is still a somewhat elitist activity: what is shared? how much knowledge is needed? why bother? and should we bother? One answer offered by Char is the distinction between the poem and poetry which he established during the Resistance: 'The poem is a furious ascension; poetry, the play of arid riverbanks' (*Feuillets d'Hypnos/ Leaves of Hypnos*). In other words, we must attend to each individual text and not to a culturally approved mode of writing. A further answer is proposed in another wartime statement: 'If the absurd reigns here on earth, I choose the absurd, the antistatic, or whatever brings me close to the possibilities of pathos and empathy. I am a man of the riverbanks – of erosion and swelling – since I cannot always be a man of the roaring stream.' These two statements articulate important thoughts on poetry, but they use the same image of the riverbanks (berges) to express radically different ideas. This does not mean that Char's poetics is incoherent or contradictory, but that he is committed to rethinking his position constantly, to maintaining it in a state of creative flux.

Char describes Heraclitus as 'this proud, stable and anxious genius who sees truth as noble and the image which reveals truth as tragic'. All that Char admires in Heraclitus is to be found in his own poetry, notably the anxiety about how one can possibly express or, more accurately, *unveil* the beauty of truth. The truth, however, for both these thinkers is neither serene not stable: like existence itself, it is a *becoming*, a discovery of harmony through and in discord, through and in struggle. Heraclitus asserts that the fundamental principle of existence is Strife (also translated as Hate or War) which is an external force and that Love is a unifying force *within* the world. These two forces are engaged in an eternal struggle which is the foundation of all becoming. The notion of struggle is crucial, in that it is a question not of a simple cycle in which Hate and Love succeed each other. It is a question of a creative co-existence of opposites: a process which, to paraphrase Char, involves both a straining towards the future and a remembering of the past.

The Ancient Greek idea of existence as flux had particular resonance for those who had experienced World Wars and had come to recognise that unity of thought is a fantasy created by the particular society in which we live. Furthermore, and crucially, the thoughts of Heraclitus, Empedocles and Parmenides have been left to us in *fragmented* form. Char is fascinated by the concept of fragmentation. For him, both life and poetry are tragically (though potentially creatively) structured and defined by splitting, by lack of coherence, by a principle of difference and constant differing, hence his insistent privileging of the individual poem over poetry. His own texts are usually brief and may appear to be separate, autonomous entities, yet there is in his work as a whole a continual interweaving of terms whereby ideas and images are re-presented and rethought. His preferred image for fragmentation is the archipelago. One of his volumes is called *La parole en archipel/ The Word as archipelago* and all his poems and images relate to each other as do the islands in an archipelago, which, though apparently, *superficially* distinct, are linked each to the other by a hidden submarine landmass. The reader thus becomes an explorer who must both scan the sea-surface of the poems and plumb the depths of the waters which separate the various texts in order to establish some kind of map of Char's work.

The archipelago is a central notion for Char, but he also uses another significant metaphor as the title for one of the poems in *Les Matinaux*, that of the cento. In Latin, a cento is a patchwork garment made of scraps of material, but the term has come to mean a poetic composition made up of passages selected from the work of great poets of the past. Most of the fragments which make up this poem were in fact written by the poet himself. However, what is most important is that they have the aphoristic quality of much Ancient Greek writing and *could have been written* by Heraclitus or Empedocles – with the difference that statements of moral philosophy are here made subjectively, in the first person. While Char is a highly individual poet, his work constantly refers back to past writers and especially to past conceptions of harmony – in order to make us think creatively about the destructively fragmented present in which we live today.

Char is sometimes described as a 'precious' poet in that he occasionally uses both unusual or highly specific words and syntactic structures that are 'old fashioned' or 'pedantic'. But he is also radically modern, even 'postmodern' in his insistent poetic use of fragmentation, collage and incorporation of references to the past. He is also above all an archaeologist of language who reminds us that words have a history, whether we know it or not, and that these words need to be found again, dug up, uncovered, resurrected... This concern with the past is not nostalgic, or at least not simply so: Char is preoccupied by the problems of absence and presence, both of these being bound up into a meditation upon time and history, and all of his work may be seen as an interrogation of the very movements and constructs that are nostalgia's. If he frequently returns to the notion that we still hold the 'old gods' within us, this does not mean that he is advocating a return to paganism or even pantheism. Rather, he is aware that the past is simultaneously gone and *present*, albeit in a fragmented and often unrecognised form. Hence for example his insistence on transcribing the language of the Provençal *Transparents* in order to remind us that even today there are those whose discourse ambiguously conjoins the metaphysical and the concrete.

For Char, poetry is necessary, *central*, in that only poetry can (dare to) speak truth. This truth is, however, not an absolute, immutable truth, but an *aletheia*. In his 1956 essay on Rimbaud, Char states categorically that 'without poetry [...] the world is and means nothing. True life, that unimpeachable colossus, finds its meaning only in the flanks of poetry.' While it is interesting that here as elsewhere he conceives of poetry as feminine (flanks) and of true life as masculine (colossus), what is crucial is that truth can be found only in an acceptance of difference and interaction, in the warring harmonies offered by poetry. Each individual poem is part of a patchwork, a fragment of an eternal and universal discourse that is half-lost to us – and so as readers we must engage in a kind of archeological activity. Char's occasional use of archaic syntax and of unfamiliar words taken from Provençal is neither elitist nor exclusive; rather it serves to remind us that we must seek to refind the original meaning of words in order to reposition ourselves fully in the present. Yes, many of us may sometimes need to use dictionaries or encyclopaedias when reading his poems, but this is part of the poet's committed strategy to make us reconsider the past so that we may re-encounter and rethink the complex simplicity of vision of our predecessors, be they pre-Socratic philosophers, clear-seeing wanderers, fisherfolk, farmers or poachers – or poets.

In his 1985 volume *Les voisinages de Van Gogh/In Van Gogh's territory*, which in its subtle and erudite allusions to Provence offers an interesting counterpoint to *Les Matinaux / The Dawn Breakers*, the vocabulary is more recondite and the references more problematic for the uninitiated reader, but the concern with the past's relation to the present is just as dominant. The first, programmatic text is called 'L'avant-Glanum'/'Before Glanum', referring to the quarry where Van Gogh was painting when he had his first serious fit of madness. But Char's allusion is more complex in that the Roman ruins for which Glanum is now famous were not discovered until the 1921 excavations, that is to say more than 30 years after Van Gogh's death. What matters for Char is that although Van Gogh could not possibly know of the subterranean ruins, his eye was that of the in-seeing artist who intuitively senses the past in the present – and so his painting created a link between the mountain's natural arch and the hidden town which would later be uncovered.

It is this complex web of past, present and future which underpins all of Char's poetry wherein origins lie not only in the past but also as future destinations. Through art we can uncover the truth of existence, the simple truth that all is complicated, that there are links between all things.

The Sovereign Conversation

Echo answers echo; everything reverberates.
GEORGES BRAQUE

Char's poetry is profoundly aware of the past which is our shared heritage, the 'common wealth' that in 'Anoukis and later Jeanne' permits him to understand that all experiences are repetitions. This is especially true of experiences of love which, though often presented as singular, as unique, have their full meaning because they are commemorations which rewrite the past in order to promise a new harmony in the future. This poetry is undoubtedly difficult in its moral and philosophical speculations and affirmations, but it also has a vigorous immediacy, precisely because it speaks of the problems and conflicts which have preoccupied human beings since time immemorial. Char is firmly, even aggressively, explicit on issues of social justice. He is however questioningly suggestive when writing about his individual emotional experiences which he perceives as simultaneously deeply personal and characteristic of all human behaviour. Our passions are not simply the product of our own psyches and libidos: they are always partially determined by the culture in which we live, hence Char's conscious and unconscious dialogue with past and present writings, paintings and music.

If the creation of poetry is necessarily a solitary and individual-istic activity, the reading of poetry is collaborative. We each bring to texts our own thoughts, hopes and especially our memories. We try out our own histories against those of the poet, and the marvel-lous miracle occurs: we recognise that what poets say reveals more about ourselves than it does about them.

When Char wrote, it was always alone, whether in the necessary solitude of every poet or in the brief 'absence' of the Resistance fighter, yet in all of his moments of creation he was accompanied by other artists with whom he silently dialogued, notably Heraclitus, Sade, Hölderlin, Rimbaud, Éluard, Heidegger, Braque, Picasso – and Georges de la Tour. Throughout the War he kept pinned to his wall a colour print of de la Tour's *The Prisoner* which depicts a woman speaking to a captive. All of de la Tour's luminescently candle-lit paintings fascinated Char but *The Prisoner* had a partic-ular significance for him during the War because, as he says, this representation of a dialogue between human beings 'defeated and brought under control the manifold darkness of Hitlerism' (*Fureur et mystère/ Furor and Mystery*). This is one of the rare examples where Char privileges the decoding of content over emotional res-ponse. Usually he strives to transcribe and to generate an experi-ence of *happening*. This happening is a form of *aletheia* whereby we discover that we both belong to the past and are different from it. In his essays on artists, he often insists on his sense of belonging (in an ambivalent way) to a tradition, and his choice of epigraphs from writers as diverse as Heraclitus, Empedocles, Shakespeare, Monteverdi, Blake and Melville further underlines his anti-historical commitment to discovery of the past as a recognition but also as a becoming, a moving-onwards. The Tradition is for Char what Paz has called a tradition of discontinuity. This explains his reluctance to write fully-argued theoretical essays, preferring to offer short aphor-istic texts which allow his readers space to interpret, to reposition themselves in time – and above all to create their own meanings.

Throughout the work of this tragic optimist, of this darkly lum-inous poet burns one constant light: the beacon of hope in our individual and collective capacity to surmount oppression. All of the Dawn Breakers, be they human or animal, are therefore to be respected and cherished, for they are our models in a world of moral poverty. Char's work may point up the gloom which shrouds contemporary existence, yet always there is a sense that progress will be made. In his 1979 volume *Fenêtres dormantes et porte sur le toit/ Sleeping windows and door on the roof*, he restates unequivocally this belief that informs all the poems in *Les Matinaux:* 'The Dawn Breakers would go on living, even if there were no more evening, no more morning.'

MICHAEL WORTON
University College London

Bibliography: Works mentioned and further reading

RENÉ CHAR: Poetry

Only those of Char's volumes not included in the *Oeuvres complètes* are given here
Les cloches sur le cœur (Paris: Le Rouge et le Noir, 1928).
Oeuvres complètes (Paris: Gallimard, 1983).
Les voisinages de Van Gogh (Paris: Gallimard, 1985).
Éloge d'une soupçonnée (Paris: Gallimard, 1988).
Poems of René Char, translated by Mary Ann Caws and Jonathan Griffin (Princeton University Press, 1976).

Critical Books on René Char

Michael Bishop: *René Char: Les dernières années* (Amsterdam: Rodopi, 1990).
Mary Ann Caws: *The Presence of René Char* (Princeton University Press, 1981).
Mechthild Cranston: *Orion Resurgent. René Char: Poet of Presence* (Madrid: Studia Humanitatis, 1979).
Christine Dupouy: *René Char* (Paris: Belfond, 1987).
Tineke Kingma-Eijgendaal and Paul J. Smith: *Lectures de René Char* (Amsterdam: CRIN/Rodopi, 1990).
Virginia La Charité: *The Poetics and the Poetry of René Char* (Chapel Hill: University of North Carolina Press, 1968).
James Lawler: *René Char: The Myth and the Poem* (Princeton University Press, 1978).
Eric Marty: *René Char* (Paris: Seuil, 1990).
Jean-Claude Mathieu: *La Poésie de René Char ou le sel et la splendeur*, 2 vols (Paris: Corti, 1984 & 1985).
Paul Veyne: *René Char en ses poèmes* (Paris: Gallimard, 1990).
World Literature Today (Focus on René Char), 1977.

Other works mentioned

Christopher Caudwell: *Illusion and Reality* (London: Lawrence and Wishart, 1946).
Martin Heidegger: *Poetry, Language, Thought*, translated by Alfred Hofstadter (New York: Harper and Row, 1971).
Octavio Paz: *Alternating Current*, translated by Helen R. Lane (London: Wildwood House, 1974).
Octavio Paz: *The Bow and the Lyre*, translated by Ruth L.C. Simms (New York: McGraw-Hill, 1973).

APEMANTUS: Where liest o'nights, Timon?

TIMON: Under that's above me.

SHAKESPEARE
Timon of Athens

FÊTE DES ARBRES ET DU CHASSEUR

CELEBRATION OF THE TREES AND THE HUNTER

Fête des arbres et du chasseur

Abrégé

Les deux joueurs de guitare sont assis sur des chaises de fer dans un décor de plein air méditerranéen. Un moment ils préludent et vérifient leur instrument. Arrive le chasseur. Il est vêtu de toile. Il porte un fusil et une gibecière. Il dit avec lenteur, la voix triste, les premiers vers du poème, accompagné tres doucement par les guitares, puis va chasser. Chaque guitariste, à tour de rôle, module la part du poème qui lui revient, en observant un silence après chaque quatrain, silence ventilé par les guitares. Un coup de feu est entendu. Le chasseur réapparaît, et comme précédemment, s'avance vers le public. Il dit l'avant-final du poème, harcelé par les guitares dont les joueurs se sont dressés et l'encadrent. Enfin les deux guitaristes chantent haut ensemble le final, le chasseur muet, tête basse, entre eux. Dans le lointain, des arbres brûlent.

Les deux guitares exaltent dans la personne du chasseur mélancolique (il tue les oiseaux «pour que l'arbre lui reste» cependant que sa cartouche met du même coup le feu à la forêt) l'exécutant d'une contradiction conforme à l'exigence de la création.

Celebration of the trees and the hunter

Summary

The two guitar-players are seated on wrought-iron chairs in an open-air Mediterranean setting. They spend a few moments warming up and tuning their instruments. The hunter arrives, wearing a canvas jacket. He is carrying a shot-gun and a gamebag. Accompanied by the soft strumming of the guitars, he speaks the first lines of the poem slowly, mournfully, then leaves to go hunting. In turn, each guitarist modulates his own parts of the poem; after each verse, they mark a pause which is ventilated by the plucking of guitar strings. A shot is heard. The hunter reappears, and as before moves downstage. As he recites the penultimate verse, he is badgered by the guitars whose players have stood up and come to stand on either side of him. Finally the two guitarists sing out the last verse as a duet, while the hunter, head bowed, stands silently between them. In the distance, trees are burning.

In the figure of the melancholy hunter (who kills the birds 'to keep the tree for himself' but at the same time sets fire to the forest with his cartridge), the two guitars celebrate the agent of a contradiction in keeping with the demands of existence.

LE CHASSEUR

Sédentaires aux ailes stridentes
Ou voyageurs du ciel profond,
Oiseaux, nous vous tuons
Pour que l'arbre nous reste et sa morne patience.

Départ du chasseur. Les guitares,
tour à tour, vont évoquer son univers.

PREMIÈRE GUITARE

Est-ce l'abord des libertés,
L'espérance d'une plaie vive,
Qu'à votre cime vous portez,
Peuplier à taille d'ogive?

DEUXIÈME GUITARE

L'enfant que vous déshabillez,
Églantier, malin des carrières,
Voit la langue de vos baisers
En transparence dans sa chair.

PREMIÈRE GUITARE

Le chien que le grelot harcèle
Gémit, aboie et lâche pied.
La magie sèche l'ensorcèle
Qui joue de son habileté.

DEUXIÈME GUITARE

Tourterelle, ma tristesse
A mon insu définie,
Ton chant est mon chant de minuit,
Ton aile bat ma forteresse.

PREMIÈRE GUITARE

Les appelants dans la froidure
Exhortent le feu du fusil
À jaillir de sa cage, lui,
Pour maintenir leur imposture.

THE HUNTER

Wing-clattering stay-at-homes,
Or wanderers through the sky-depths,
Birds, we kill you
To keep for ourselves the tree and its long-suffering gloom.

*Exit the hunter. The guitars take turns
to evoke his universe.*

FIRST GUITAR

The approaches of freedom,
The hope of an open wound,
Are these what we find at your top,
High vaulted poplar tree?

SECOND GUITAR

Dog-rose, sly spirit of the quarries,
The child you strip bare
Sees the tongue-marks of your kisses
Printed clearly in his flesh.

FIRST GUITAR

The dog badgered by the bell
Whines, barks and gives ground.
Dry magic binds it with a spell,
Playing on all its skill.

SECOND GUITAR

Turtledove, my secret sadness
Still hidden from me,
Your song is my midnight serenade,
Your wing beats at my fortress.

FIRST GUITAR

The decoy-birds sitting in the cold
Urge the gun-fire to spurt forth
From its cage in order to protect
Their false identities.

DEUXIÈME GUITARE

Le chêne et le gui se murmurent
Les projets de leurs ennemis,
Le bûcheron aux hanches dures,
La faucille de l'enfant chétif.

PREMIÈRE GUITARE

La panacée de l'incendie,
Mantes, sur vos tiges cassantes,
Porte l'éclair dans votre nuit,
En vue de vos amours violentes.

DEUXIÈME GUITARE

Dors dans le creux de ma main,
Olivier, en terre nouvelle;
C'est sûr, la journée sera belle
Malgré l'entame du matin.

*Coup de fusil dans la forêt et
son echo jusqu'aux guitares.*

PREMIÈRE GUITARE

L'alouette à peine éclairée
Scintille et crée le souhait qu'elle chante;
Et la terre des affamés
Rampe vers cette vivante.

DEUXIÈME GUITARE

On marche, on brise son chemin,
On taille avec un couteau aigre
Un bâton pour réduire enfin
La grande fatigue des pères.

PREMIÈRE GUITARE

Cyprès que le chasseur blesse
Dans l'hallucination du soir clair,
Entre la lumière et la mer
Tombent vos chaudes silhouettes.

54

SECOND GUITAR

The oak and the mistletoe whisper to each other
The plans of their enemies:
The firm-thighed woodcutter
And the puny child's sickle.

FIRST GUITAR

Mantises perched on your brittle stalks:
The panacea of the forest-fire
Flashes lightning into your darkness,
With your violent love-making in mind.

SECOND GUITAR

Sleep in the palm of my hand,
Olive tree, sleep in new earth;
It's sure to be a beautiful day
Despite the heel sliced from morning.

*A gun-shot sounds in the forest,
echoing through to the guitars.*

FIRST GUITAR

Lit briefly by dawn's rays, the lark
Flashes and creates the hope it sings;
And the starveling world of men
Crawls up to meet this living thing.

SECOND GUITAR

We walk, we blaze our trails,
And with bitter-sharp knives carve
Staffs that shall finally ease
The weariness of our old men.

FIRST GUITAR

Cypress trees that the hunter scars
In the mirage formed by the radiant evening,
Between the sunlight and the sea
Fall your warm, dark shadows.

DEUXIÈME GUITARE

Si l'on perd de vue ses querelles,
On échange aussi sa maison
Contre un rocher dont l'horizon
S'égoutte sous une fougère

PREMIÈRE GUITARE

Chère ombre que nous vénérons
Dans les calendes d'errants,
Rangez les herbes que défont
La nuque et les doigts des amants.

DEUXIÈME GUITARE

Le cœur s'éprend d'un ruisseau clair,
Y jette sa cartouche amère.
Il feint d'ignorer que la mer
Lui recédera le mystere.

PREMIÈRE GUITARE

Douleur et temps flânent ensemble.
Quelle volonté les assemble?
Prenez, hirondelles atones,
Confidence de leur personne.

DEUXIÈME GUITARE

Aimez, lorsque volent les pierres
Sous la foulée de votre pas,
Chasseur, le carré de lumière
Qui marque leur place ici-bas.

Retour du chasseur.

LE CHASSEUR

Il faut nous voir marcher dans cet ennui de vous,
Forêt qui subsistez dans l'émotion de tous,
A distance des portes, à peine reconnue.
Devant l'étincelle du vide,
Vous n'êtes jamais seule, ô grande disparue!

SECOND GUITAR

If you lose sight of your quarrels,
You also exchange your house
For a rock whose horizon
Drips down under a fern.

FIRST GUITAR

Sweet shade that we worship
On New Year's Day when spirits return,
Tidy the grass rumpled by
The necks and fingers of lovers.

SECOND GUITAR

The heart falls in love with a radiant stream,
Tosses in its acrid cartridge,
Feigning not to know that the sea
Will return the mystery one day.

FIRST GUITAR

Time and suffering stroll arm in arm.
What power brings them together?
Listen closely, atonic swallows,
To the secrets their bodies display.

SECOND GUITAR

Hunter, when the stones fly up
From under your striding feet,
You should love the square of light
That marks their place on this earth.

The hunter returns.

THE HUNTER

You should see us walk and mourn for you,
Forest still alive in our fluttering hearts,
Far from our doors, barely known.
When faced with the spark of the void,
You are never alone, O great vanished one!

LES GUITARES

Merci, et la Mort s'étonne;
Merci, la Mort n'insiste pas;
Merci, c'est le jour qui s'en va;
Merci simplement à un homme
S'il tient en échec le glas.

The flames of the burning forest are seen in the distance.

THE GUITARS

Thank you, and Death is surprised;
Thank you, Death does not insist;
Thank you, it is day departing;
Thank you simply to a man
If he keeps the knell at bay.

LA SIESTE BLANCHE
THE SLEEPLESS SIESTA

Mise en garde

Nous avons sur notre versant tempéré une suite de chansons *qui nous flanquent, ailes de communication entre notre souffle reposé et nos fièvres les plus fortes. Pièces presque banales, d'un coloris clément, d'un contour arriéré, dont le tissu cependant porte une minuscule plaie. Il est loisible à chacun de fixer une origine et un terme à cette* rougeur *contestable.*

En un temps où la mort, docile aux faux sorciers, souille les chances les plus hautes, nous n'hésitons pas à mettre en liberté *tous les instants dont nous disposons. Ou mieux, qu'on se tourne vers l'ipomée, ce liseron que l'heure ultime de la nuit raffine et entrouvre, mais que midi condamne à se fermer. Il serait extraordinaire que la quiétude au revers de laquelle précairement il nous accueille, ne fût pas celle que nous avions, pour une sieste, souhaitée.*

Warning

As we live and walk on our temperate slopes, we are escorted by a series of songs, *wings of communication between our fiercest fevers and our moments of rest: almost banal fragments, mildly coloured and dated in their form, their fabric nonetheless pierced by a tiny wound. Everyone has the freedom to set their own beginning and end to this ambiguous* redness.

In an age when death, the plaything of false sorcerers, soils our highest hopes, we have no hesitation in liberating *all the fleeting moments at our disposal. Or still better, let us turn to the moon-flower, that bindweed which, polished and half-opened by the final hour of night, is condemned to closure by noon. It is inconceivable that the peace where we are precariously welcomed under the leaf be not that very peace that we had desired – for our siesta.*

Divergence

Le cheval à la tête étroite
A condamné son ennemi,
Le poète aux talons oisifs,
A de plus sévères zéphyrs
Que ceux qui courent dans sa voix.
La terre ruinée se reprend
Bien qu'un fer continu la blesse.

Rentrez aux fermes, gens patients;
Sur les amandiers au printemps
Ruissellent vieillesse et jeunesse.
La mort sourit au bord du temps
Qui lui donne quelque noblesse.

C'est sur les hauteurs de l'été
Que le poète se révolte,
Et du brasier de la récolte
Tire sa torche et sa folie.

Divergence

The narrow-headed horse
Has condemned his enemy,
The lazy-heeled poet,
To harsher zephyrs
Than those coursing through his voice.
The ruined earth revives
Though wounded by unceasing blades.

Return to your farms, patient folk;
Over the almond trees in spring
Stream old age and youth.
Death smiles on the edge of time
That gives it some nobility.

There on the heights of summer
The poet strikes his revolt
And draws from the harvest's furnace
Both his torch and his folly.

Complainte du lézard amoureux

N'égraine pas le tournesol,
Tes cyprès auraient de la peine,
Chardonneret, reprends ton vol
Et reviens à ton nid de laine.

Tu n'es pas un caillou du ciel
Pour que le vent te tienne quitte,
Oiseau rural; l'arc-en-ciel
S'unifie dans la marguerite.

L'homme fusille, cache-toi;
Le tournesol est son complice.
Seules les herbes sont pour toi,
Les herbes des champs qui se plissent.

Le serpent ne te connaît pas,
Et la sauterelle est bougonne;
La taupe, elle, n'y voit pas;
Le papillon ne hait personne.

Il est midi, chardonneret.
Le séneçon est là qui brille.
Attarde-toi, va, sans danger:
L'homme est rentré dans sa famille!

L'écho de ce pays est sur.
J'observe, je suis bon prophète;
Je vois tout de mon petit mur,
Même tituber la chouette.

Qui, mieux qu'un lézard amoureux,
Peut dire les secrets terrestres?
Ô léger gentil roi des cieux,
Que n'as-tu ton nid dans ma pierre!

Orgon, août 1947

66

Lament of the love-sick lizard

Don't pick all the sunflower's seeds,
Your cypress trees would be sad,
Goldfinch, take to your wings again
And return to your nest of wool.

You're no pebble stuck in the sky
The wind would go passing by,
Country bird; in the daisy
The rainbow finds its unity.

The man is out shooting, so hide;
The sunflower is his accomplice.
Only the grasses are on your side,
The field-grasses that furrow and fold.

The snake does not greet you,
And the grasshopper is grumpy;
The mole, of course, sees nothing;
The butterfly hates nobody.

It is noon now, goldfinch.
There's the groundsel, shining bright.
Stay a while, do stay, you're safe now:
The man has returned to his family!

The echoes here ring true.
I keep watch, I prophesy well;
I see everything from my low wall,
Even the teeterings of the owl.

Who better than a love-sick lizard
Can tell the secrets of the earth?
O light kindly king of the skies,
Why not nest in my stone!

Orgon, August 1947

Les Transparents

Les Transparents *ou vagabonds luni-solaires ont de nos jours à peu près complètement disparu des bourgs et des forêts où on avait coutume de les apercevoir. Affables et déliés, ils dialoguaient en vers avec l'habitant, le temps de déposer leur besace et de la reprendre. L'habitant, l'imagination émue, leur accordait le pain, le vin, le sel et l'oignon cru; s'il pleuvait, la paille.*

I. *Toquebiol*

L'HABITANT

– Travaille, une ville naîtra
Où chaque logis sera ton logis.

TOQUEBIOL

– Innocence, ton vœu finit
Sur la faucille de mon pas.

II. *Laurent de Venasque*

Laurent se plaint. Sa maîtresse n'est pas venue au rendezvous. Dépité, il s'en va.

À trop attendre,
On perd sa foi.

Celui qui part
N'est point menteur.

Ah! le voyage,
Petite source.

The Clear-seeing

The Clear-seeing Ones *or lunisolar vagabonds have now almost all disappeared from the towns and forests where we used to catch sight of them. Affable and quick of tongue, they would chat in verse with the locals while they caught their breath between setting down and picking up their packs. The imagination of the locals was fired; they would give them bread, wine, salt and raw onions – and if it rained, a bed in the byre.*

I. *Toquebiol*

THE LOCAL

Work, and we shall build a town
Where each house will be your home.

TOQUEBIOL

Silly fool, your wish ends
On the sickle of my footsteps.

II. *Laurent de Venasque*

*Laurent is singing a lament. His beloved has not come
to the tryst. He leaves in pique.*

Waiting too long
Makes one lose faith.

He who leaves
Is in no way a liar.

Ah! journeying,
A mountain-spring.

III. *Pierre Prieuré*

PIERRE

– Prononce un vœu, nuit où je vois?

LA NUIT

– Que le rossignol se taise,
Et l'impossible amour qu'il veut calme en son cœur.

IV. *Églin Ambrozane*

LA GALANTE

– Commencez à vous réjouir,
Étranger, je vais vous ouvrir.

ÉGLIN

– Je suis le loup chagrin,
Beauté, pour vous servir.

III. *Pierre Prieuré*

PIERRE

Will you make a wish, O night in which I see?

THE NIGHT

Let the nightingale be silent,
And the impossible love she would have calm in her heart.

IV. *Églin Ambrozane*

THE FLIRT

Start your rejoicing,
Stranger, I'll open my door to you.

ÉGLIN

I am the sorrowful wolf,
Pretty one, at your service.

V. *Diane Cancel*

LE CASANIER

– Les tuiles de bonne cuisson,
Des murs moulés comme des arches,
Les fenêtres en proportion,
Le lit en merisier de Sparte,
Un miroir de flibusterie
Pour la Rose de mon souci.

DIANE

– Mais la clé, qui tourne deux fois
Dans ta porte de patriarche,
Souffle l'ardeur, éteint la voix.
Sur le talus, l'amour quitté, le vent m'endort.

VI. *René Mazon*

Le rocher parle par la bouche de René.

Je suis la première pierre de la volonte de Dieu, le rocher;
L'indigent de son jeu et le moins belliqueux.

Figuier, pénètre-moi:
Mon apparence est un défi, ma profondeur une amitié.

VII. *Jacques Aiguillée*

Jacques se peint.

Quand tout le monde prie,
Nous sommes incrédules.
Quand personne n'a foi,
Nous devenons croyants.
Tel l'œil du chat, nous varions.

V. *Diane Cancel*

THE STAY-AT-HOME

The well-fired tiles,
Walls moulded like arches,
The well-proportioned windows,
The bed of Spartan cherry-wood,
A free-booting mirror
For the Rose of my heart's care.

DIANE

But the key, which turns twice
To lock your patriarchal door,
Snuffs out passion, silences speech.
On the river-bank, when love is done, the wind lulls me to sleep.

VI. *René Mazon*

René is the mouth-piece for the rock.

I am the cornerstone of God's will, the rock;
The pauper-pawn in His game and the least bellicose.

Fig tree, penetrate me:
My surface is a challenge, my depth friendship.

VII. *Jacques Aiguillée*

Jacques is painting a self-portrait.

When everyone prays,
I remain sceptical.
When no one has faith,
I become a believer.
Like a cat's eye, I change.

VIII. *Odin le Roc*

Ce qui vous fascine par endroit dans mon vers, c'est l'avenir, glissante obscurité d'avant l'aurore, tandis que la nuit est au passé déjà.

Les mille métiers se ressemblent;
Tous les ruisseaux coulent ensemble,
Bande d'incorrigibles chiens,
Malgré vos oreilles qui tremblent
Sur le tourment de votre chaîne.
Le juron de votre seigneur
Est une occasion de poussière,
Bêtes, qui durcissez le pain
Dans la maigreur de l'herbe.

*

Que les gouttes de pluie soient en toute saison
Les beaux éclairs de l'horizon:
La terre nous la parcourons.
Matin, nous lui baisons le front.

Chaque femme se détournant,
Notre chance c'est d'obtenir
Que la foudre en tombant devienne
L'incendie de notre plaisir.

Tourterelle, oiseau de noblesse,
L'orage oublie qui le traverse.

IX. *Joseph Puissantseigneur*

JOSEPH

Route, es-tu la?

MOI

Les prodigues s'en vont ensemble.

74

VIII. *Odin le Roc*

What fascinates you here and there in my verses is the future,
a shifting darkness before dawn, when night is already gone.

All jobs are the same;
All streams run together,
Pack of refractory dogs,
Even though your ears twitch
As your chains torment you.
Your master's curse
Can make the dust fly,
Beasts, you who harden the bread
In the sparseness of the grass.

*

In every season may the raindrops be
Beautiful lightning flashes on the horizon;
We travel and scour the earth.
In the morning, we kiss its brow.

Since every woman turns away,
We can only hope to ensure
That the lightning-strike becomes
The forest-fire of our pleasure.

Turtledove, bird of nobility,
The storm forgets who flies through it.

IX. *Joseph Puissantseigneur*

JOSEPH

Road, are you there?

MOI

The extravagant leave together.

X. *Gustave Chamier*

Écoutez passer, regardez partir
De votre fierté si longue à fléchir,
La paille du grain qui ne peut pourrir.
Faible est le grenier que le pain méprise.

XI. *Étienne Fage*

J'éveille mon amour
Pour qu'il me dise l'aube,
La défaite de tous.

XII. *Aimeri Favier*

AIMERI

– Vous enterrez le vent,
Ami, en m'enterrant.

LE FOSSOYEUR

– Qu'importe où va le vent!
Mais sa bêche resta dedans.

X. *Gustave Chamier*

Listen to the passing, see the parting
From your stubbornly resistant pride
Of the chaff that shall never rot.
Weak is the corn-loft that's scorned by the bread.

XI. *Étienne Fage*

I waken my love
To be told it is dawn,
The time when all are vanquished.

XII. *Aimeri Favier*

AIMERI

You bury the wind,
Friend, when you bury me.

THE GRAVEDIGGER

Who cares where the wind goes!
But its spade stayed planted there.

XIII. *Louis le Bel*

LOUIS

– Brûleurs de ronces, enragés jardiniers,
Vous êtes mes pareils, mais que vous m'écœurez!

LES TACHERONS

– Batteur de taches de soleil,
Nous sommes surmenés, nous sommes satisfaits.
Que répondre à cela,
Vieil enfant?

LOUIS

– Le cœur aidant l'effort,
Marcher jusqu'à la mort
Qui clôt la liberté
Qui laissait l'illusion.

XIV. *Jean Jaume*

JEAN

L'olivier, à moi, m'est jumeau,
Ô bleu de l'air, ô bleu corbeau!
Quelques collines se le dirent,
Et les senteurs se confondirent.

XIII. *Louis le Bel*

LOUIS

Bramble burners, mad-keen gardeners,
You're my brothers, but how you disgust me!

THE PIECEWORKERS

Thresher of sunspots,
We are overworked, we are content.
What reply can you make to that,
Aged child?

LOUIS

With your heart's help, strive
To walk all the way to death
That closes off the freedom
That left behind illusion.

XIV. *Jean Jaume*

JEAN

The olive tree is, I know, my twin,
O blue of the air, O raven blue!
Some hills told each other this,
And all scents merged into one.

XV. *Comte de Sault*

Son epitaphe:

Aux lourdes roses assombries,
Désir de la main des aveugles,
Préfère, passant, l'églantier
Dont je suis la pointe amoureuse
Qui survit à ton effusion.

XVI. *Claude Palun*

LE PAYSAN

– Nul ne croit qu'il meurt pour de bon,
S'il regarde la gerbe au soir de la moisson
Et la verse du grain dans sa main lui sourire.

CLAUDE

– Diligent, nous te dépassons,
Notre éternité est de givre.

XVII. *Albert Ensénada*

Le monde où les Transparents *vivaient et qu'ils aimaient,
prend fin. Albert le sait.*

Les fusils chargés nous remplacent
Et se tait l'aboiement des chiens.
Apparaissez formes de glace,
Nous, *Transparents*, irons plus loin.

XV. *Comte de Sault*

His epitaph:

To the heavy, darkened roses
Sought by the hands of the blind,
Prefer, O passer-by, the dog-rose:
I am its loving thorn
That survives all your effusions.

XVI. *Claude Palun*

THE PEASANT

No man believes that his death is a final end,
If after a day's harvesting he sees the sheaves shine
And the grain smile as it pours into his hand.

CLAUDE

Diligent worker, our faith is greater than yours:
Our eternity is made of frost.

XVII. *Albert Ensénada*

The world loved and inhabited by the Clear-seeing Ones
is coming to an end. Albert knows this.

The loaded guns replace us
And the dogs' barking is done.
Appear, take shape, forms of ice,
We, the *Clear-seeing Ones*, are set to move on.

Jouvence des Névons

Dans l'enceinte du parc, le grillon ne
se tait que pour s'établir davantage.

Dans le parc des Névons
Ceinturé de prairies,
Un ruisseau sans talus,
Un enfant sans ami
Nuancent leur tristesse
Et vivent mieux ainsi.

Dans le parc des Névons
Un rebelle s'est joint
Au ruisseau, à l'enfant,
À leur mirage enfin.

Dans le parc des Névons
Mortel serait l'été
Sans la voix d'un grillon
Qui, par instant, se tait.

Youth at Les Névons

Within the walls of the grounds, the cricket's occasional
silence is just its way of making itself really heard.

In the grounds of Les Névons
Surrounded by fields,
A stream without banks
And a child without friends
Shade all their sadness
And live better thus.

In the grounds of Les Névons
A rebel has joined forces
With the stream, with the child,
Or rather with their mirage.

In the grounds of Les Névons
The summer would be lethal
Without the chirp of a cricket
Which, sometimes, falls silent.

Hermétiques ouvriers...

Hermétiques ouvriers
En guerre avec mon silence,

Même le givre vous offense
À la vitre associé!
Même une bouche que j'embrasse
Sur sa muette fierté!

Partout j'entends implorer grâce
Puis rugir et déferler,
Fugitifs devant la torche,
Agonie demain buisson.

Dans la ville où elle existe,
La foule s'enfièvre déjà.
La lumière qui lui ment
Est un tambour dans l'espace.

Aux épines du torrent
Ma laine maintient ma souffrance.

Hermetic workers...

Hermetic workers
At war with my silence,

Even the frost insults you,
Colluding with the window-pane!
Even the mouth that I kiss
On its silent pride!

On all sides I hear cries for mercy
Then a roaring and unfurling,
Fugitives fleeing before the torch,
Dying tomorrow blossoms as a bush.

In the town where they live,
The masses are already inflamed.
The light that deceives them
Is a drum beating in the void.

On the thorns of the torrent
My wool maintains my suffering.

Conseil de la sentinelle

Fruit qui jaillissez du couteau,
Beauté dont saveur est l'écho,
Aurore à gueule de tenailles,
Amants qu'on veut désassembler,
Femme qui portez tablier,
Ongle qui grattez la muraille,
Désertez! désertez!

The guard's advice

Fruit spurting under the knife's cut,
Beauty savoured best when echoed,
Dawn that bites like a vice,
Lovers whom men seek to separate,
Woman wearing an apron,
Fingernail scratching the wall:
You must all desert! Desert!

Corail

À un Othello

Il s'alarme a l'idée que, le regard appris,
Il ne reste des yeux que l'herbe du mensonge.
Il est si méfiant que son auvent se gâte
À n'attendre que lui seul.

Nul n'empêche jamais la lumière exilée
De trouver son élu dans l'inconnu surpris.
Elle franchit d'un bond l'espace et le jaloux,
Et c'est un astre entier de plus.

Coral

To an Othello

He suddenly fears that, once he has learned to see,
His eyes just weeds of betrayal.
He is so suspicious that his porch is overgrown
From expecting no one but him to come.

No one can ever stop exiled light
From finding its Chosen One in a stranger taken unawares.
It leaps across both space and the jealous lover –
And another complete star is created.

Pyrénées

Montagne des grands abusés,
Au sommet de vos tours fiévreuses
Faiblit la dernière clarté.

Rien que le vide et l'avalanche,
La détresse et le regret!

Tous ces troubadours mal-aimés
Ont vu blanchir dans un été
Leur doux royaume pessimiste.

Ah! la neige est inexorable
Qui aime qu'on souffre à ses pieds,
Qui veut que l'on meure glacé
Quand on a vécu dans les sables.

Pyrenees

Mountain range of the great misled,
Your fevered towers are capped
By the last fading rays of light.

Only chasm and avalanche,
Anguish and regret!

All the minstrels of doomed love
Have seen, in one summer, the blanching of
Their sweet but hopeless kingdom.

Ah! merciless is the snow
Which loves us to suffer at its feet,
Which wants us to freeze to death
When we have lived in sand-dunes.

Qu'il vive!

Ce pays n'est qu'un vœu de l'esprit, un contre-sepulcre.

Dans mon pays, les tendres preuves du printemps et les oiseaux mal habillés sont préférés aux buts lointains.

La vérité attend l'aurore à côté d'une bougie. Le verre de fenêtre est négligé. Qu'importe à l'attentif.

Dans mon pays, on ne questionne pas un homme ému.

Il n'y a pas d'ombre maligne sur la barque chavirée.

Bonjour à peine, est inconnu dans mon pays.

On n'emprunte que ce qui peut se rendre augmenté.

Il y a des feuilles, beaucoup de feuilles sur les arbres de mon pays. Les branches sont libres de n'avoir pas de fruits.

On ne croit pas à la bonne foi du vainqueur.

Dans mon pays, on remercie.

My land forever!

This region is only a mental image, a counter to entombment.

In my region, we prefer the tender proofs of spring and birds in tattered costume to distant goals.

Truth waits for dawn by the light of a candle. The window-pane is dirty. The watcher does not care.

In my region, we never question a deeply moved man.

There are no baneful shadows cast over the capsized boat.

Casual greetings are unknown in my region.

We borrow only what we can give back with interest.

There are leaves, many leaves, on the trees in my region. The branches are free to bear no fruit.

We do not trust the victor's word.

In my region, we say thank you.

Cet amour à tous retiré

Sur la terre de la veille
La foudre était pure au ruisseau,
La vigne sustentait l'abeille,
L'épaule levait le fardeau.

Les routes flânaient, leur poussière
Avec les oiseaux s'envolait,
Les pierres s'ajoutaient aux pierres,
Des mains utiles les aimaient.

Du moins à chaque heure souffrante
Un écho devait répéter
Pour la solitude ignorante
Un grêle devoir d'amitié.

La violence était magique,
L'homme quelquefois mourait,
Mais à l'instant de l'agonie,
Un trait d'ambre scellait ses yeux.

Les regrets, les basses portes
Ne sont que des inductions
Pour incliner nos illusions
Et rafraîchir nos peaux mortes.

Ah! crions au vent qui nous porte
Que c'est nous qui le soulevons.
Sur la terre de tant d'efforts,
L'avantage au vaillant mensonge
Est la franche consolation!

This love lost to all

In the land of yesterday
The lightning shone in the stream,
The vine nourished the bee,
Shoulders lifted their burdens.

The roads meandered, their dust
Flew off with the birds,
Stone was placed on stone,
Each one loved by the dykers' hands.

At least whenever men suffered
An echo was there to repeat
For those in solitude and silence
A spindly commitment to friendship.

The violence was magical,
A man sometimes died,
But as death seized him,
A trace of amber would seal his eyes.

Regrets and low doors
Are only initiations
Which encourage our illusions
And revitalise our dead skins.

Ah! we should cry to the wind that bears us
That we, yes we raise that wind.
On the earth where life is all toil,
The advantage gained from lying valiantly
Is a candid consolation for us!

Sur les hauteurs

Attends encore que je vienne
Fendre le froid qui nous retient.

Nuage, en ta vie aussi menacée que la mienne.

(Il y avait un précipice dans notre maison.
C'est pourquoi nous sommes partis et nous sommes établis ici.)

On the heights

Wait a while until I come
To cleave the cold which holds us.

Cloud, in your life as threatened as mine.

(There was a precipice in our house.
So we left and set up home here.)

Dédale

Pioche! enjoignait la virole.
Saigne! répétait le couteau.
Et l'on m'arrachait la mémoire,
On martyrisait mon chaos.

Ceux qui m'avaient aimé,
Puis détesté, puis oublié,
Se penchaient à nouveau sur moi.
Certains pleuraient, d'autres étaient contents.

Sœur froide, herbe de l'hiver,
En marchant, je t'ai vue grandir,
Plus haute que mes ennemis,
Plus verte que mes souvenirs.

Labyrinth

'Dig!' enjoined the ferrule.
'Bleed!' repeated the knife.
And my memory was torn from me,
My chaos was martyred.

Those who had loved me,
Then hated, then forgotten me
Bent over me once more.
Some wept, others were pleased.

Cold sister, winter grass,
As I walked, I saw you grow,
Higher than my enemies,
Greener than my memories.

Le permissionnaire

L'ogre qui est partout:
Sur le visage qu'on attend
Et dans le languir qu'on en a,
Dans la migration des oiseaux,
Sous leur feinte tranquillité;
L'ogre qui sert chacun de nous
Et n'est jamais remercié,
Dans la maison qu'on s'est construite
Malgré la migraine du vent;
L'ogre couvert et chimérique;
Ah! s'il pouvait nous confier
Qu'il est le valet de la Mort.

The soldier on leave

The ogre who is everywhere:
On the face we wait for
And in the impatience we feel,
In the migration of birds,
Beneath their feigned calmness;
The ogre who serves each of us
And is never thanked,
In the house we built
Despite the wind's migraine;
The masked, chimerical ogre;
Ah! if only he could admit to us
That he is Death's henchman.

La vérité vous rendra libres

Tu es lampe, tu es nuit;
Cette lucarne est pour ton regard,
Cette planche pour ta fatigue,
Ce peu d'eau pour ta soif,
Les murs entiers sont à celui que ta clarté met au monde,
Ô détenue, ô Mariée!

Le tout ensemble

Faucille qui persévérez dans le ciel désuni
Malgré le jour et notre frénésie.
Lune qui nous franchis et côtoies notre cœur,
Lui, resté dans la nuit.
Liens que rien n'interrompt
Sous le talon actif, par les midis glacés.

Déjà là, printanier crépuscule!
Nous n'étions qu'éveillés, nous n'avons pas agi.

Truth will make you free

You are lamp, you are night;
This skylight is for your eyes,
This plank for your weariness,
This drop of water for your thirst,
The intact walls are for the man born of your brightness,
O prisoner, O Bride!

Everything – together

Sickle persevering in the dissolving sky
Despite dawn-light, despite our frenzy.
Moon crossing us and skirting our hearts
Which remain in darkness.
Bonds that remain intact
Though heels march on, and noon is frozen.

You're here already, spring twilight!
We were only just awake, we have not taken action.

À la désespérade

Ce puits d'eau douce au goût sauvagin qui est mer ou rien.

– Je ne désire plus que tu me sois ouvert,
Et que l'eau grelottant sous ta face profonde
Me parvienne joyeuse et douce, touffue et sombre,
(Passagères serrées accourues sur mes lèvres
Où réussissent si complètement les larmes),
Puits de mémoire, ô cœur, en repli et luttant.

– Laisse dormir ton ancre tout au fond de mon sable,
Sous l'ouragan de sel où ta tête domine,
Poète confondant, et sois heureux,
Car je m'attache encore à tes préparatifs de traversée!

At the Désespérade

This well of fresh water tasting of wildfowl is an ocean or nothing at all.

'No longer do I want you to be open for me,
Or want the water shivering below your deep surface
To come up to me, joyous and sweet, dense and dark,
(In a thick spray of drops travelling straight to my lips
Where tears triumph so absolutely),
Well of memory, O heart, in retreat and fighting.'

'Let your anchor sleep deep in my sands,
Beneath the salt-storm where your head reigns,
Poet of fusion – and be happy,
For your preparations for crossing are still my concern!'

Montagne déchirée

Oh! la toujours plus rase solitude
Des larmes qui montent aux cimes.

Quand se déclare la débâcle
Et qu'un vieil aigle sans pouvoir
Voit revenir son assurance,
Le bonheur s'élance à son tour,
À flanc d'abîme les rattrape.

Chasseur rival, tu n'as rien appris,
Toi qui sans hâte me dépasses
Dans la mort que je contredis.

Le Rébanqué, Lagnes, 29 août 1949

Torn mountain

Oh! the ever barer solitude
Of tears welling up to the peaks.

When disaster occurs
And an old, impotent eagle
Sees his confidence return,
Happiness decides it might leap forth –
And catches them before they disappear.

Rival hunter, you've learned nothing,
You who run casually past me
Into the death that I deny.

Le Rébanqué, Lagnes, 29 August 1949

Le carreau

Pures pluies, femmes attendues,
La face que vous essuyez,
De verre voué aux tourments
Est la face du révolté;
L'autre, la vitre de l'heureux,
Frissonne devant le feu de bois.

Je vous aime mystères jumeaux,
Je touche à chacun de vous;
J'ai mal et je suis léger.

The window-pane

Pure rain, women who're expected,
The surface you wash –
Glass destined to suffer –
Is the face of the rebel;
The other, the happy man's window,
Shimmers in the log-fire's light.

I love you both, mysterious twins,
I touch each of you;
I suffer, I'm in pain and I am float.

Les nuits justes

Avec un vent plus fort,
Une lampe moins obscure,
Nous devons trouver la halte
Où la nuit dira «Passez»;
Et nous saurons que c'est vrai
Quand le verre s'éteindra.

Ô terre devenue tendre!
Ô branche où mûrit ma joie!
La gueule du ciel est blanche.
Ce qui miroite, là, c'est toi,
Ma chute, mon amour, mon saccage.

The just nights

When the wind blows stronger,
When the lamp-light is dimmed,
We must find the stopping-place
Where night will say 'Go on';
And we shall know this is right
When the window goes dark.

O earth now tender!
O branch where my joy ripens!
The sky's maw is white.
The gleam up there is you,
My fall, my love, my devastation.

LE CONSENTEMENT TACITE
THE TACIT AGREEMENT

L'amoureuse en secret

Elle a mis le couvert et mené à la perfection ce à quoi son amour assis en face d'elle parlera bas tout à l'heure, en la dévisageant. Cette nourriture semblable à l'anche d'un hautbois.

Sous la table, ses chevilles nues caressent à présent la châleur du bien-aimé, tandis que des voix qu'elle n'entend pas la complimentent. Le rayon de la lampe emmêle, tisse sa distraction sensuelle.

Un lit, très loin, sait-elle, patiente et tremble dans l'exil des draps odorants, comme un lac de montagne qui ne sera jamais abandonné.

Loving him secretly

She has laid the table and perfectly prepared all that her lover will address softly later when, seated opposite her, he gazes at her. This food resonant as an oboe-reed.

For the moment, her bare ankles are content to stroke the warm flesh of her beloved, while other, unheard voices compliment her. The lamp's light entangles and weaves its sensual distraction.

A far-off bed, she knows, is waiting, trembling in the exile of sweet-smelling sheets, like a mountain-lake which can never be left or forgotten.

L'adolescent souffleté

Les mêmes coups qui l'envoyaient au sol le lançaient en même temps loin devant sa vie, vers les futures années où, quand il saignerait, ce ne serait plus à cause de l'iniquité d'un seul. Tel l'arbuste que réconfortent ses racines et qui presse ses rameaux meurtris contre son fût résistant, il descendait ensuite à reculons dans le mutisme de ce savoir et dans son innocence. Enfin il s'échappait, s'enfuyait et devenait souverainement heureux. Il atteignait la prairie et la barrière des roseaux dont il cajolait la vase et percevait le sec frémissement. Il semblait que ce que la terre avait produit de plus noble et de plus persévérant, l'avait, en compensation, adopté.

Il recommencerait ainsi jusqu'au moment où, la nécessité de rompre disparue, il se tiendrait droit et attentif parmi les hommes, à la fois plus vulnérable et plus fort.

The slapped adolescent

Those same blows which felled him to the ground projected him far ahead into his life, towards the future years when his bleeding would no longer be caused by any single act of cruelty. Like a shrub which, comforted by its roots, presses its bruised boughs against its strong trunk, he would then retreat, backwards, into the silence of this knowledge – and into innocence. Finally he would escape, flee, and become sovereignly happy. He would reach the meadow and hedge of reeds whose silt he coaxed, whose dry rustling he noted and heard. He could feel that the most noble and enduring of Earth's creations had adopted him – as if to make amends.

So he would begin again and again until the time came when he no longer needed to break away and could take his place among men: standing upright, aware of others' needs, both stronger and more vulnerable.

Grège

La Fête, c'est le ciel d'un bleu belliqueux et à la même seconde le temps au précipité orageux. C'est un risque dont le regard nous suit et nous maintient, soit qu'il nous interpelle, soit qu'il se ravise. C'est le grand emportement contre un ordre avantageux pour en faire jaillir un amour…Et sortir vainqueur de la Fête, c'est, lorsque cette main sur notre épaule nous murmure: «Pas si vite…», cette main dont l'équivoque s'efforce de retarder le retour à la mort, de se jeter dans l'irréalisable de la Fête.

Grège

A Celebration is both a bellicose blue sky and a season of stormy rain. A risk whose gaze follows and sustains us, whether it calls out to us or decides to remain silent. The passionate refusal of profitable systems so that love may suddenly be born... And in order to emerge triumphantly from the Celebration we must, when the hand on our shoulder murmurs 'Not so fast...' (that hand which ambiguously and dubiously strives to delay the return to death), throw ourselves forward into the impossibility of Celebration.

Anoukis et plus tard Jeanne

Je te découvrirai à ceux que j'aime, comme un long éclair de châleur, aussi inexplicablement que tu t'es montrée à moi, Jeanne, quand, un matin s'astreignant à ton dessein, tu nous menas de roc en roc jusqu'à cette fin de soi qu'on appelle un sommet. Le visage à demi masqué par ton bras replié, les doigts de ta main sollicitant ton épaule, tu nous offris, au terme de notre ascension, une ville, les souffrances et la qualification d'un génie, la surface égarée d'un désert, et le tournant circonspect d'un fleuve sur la rive duquel des bâtisseurs s'interrogeaient. Mais je te suis vite revenu, Faucille, car tu consumais ton offrande. Et ni le temps, ni la beauté, ni le hasard qui débride le cœur ne pouvaient se mesurer avec toi.

J'ai ressuscité alors mon antique richesse, notre richesse à tous, et dominant ce que demain détruira, je me suis souvenu qui tu étais Anoukis l'Étreigneuse, aussi fantastiquement que tu étais Jeanne, la sœur de mon meilleur ami, et aussi inexplicablement que tu étais l'Étrangère dans l'esprit de ce misérable carillonneur dont le père répétait autrefois que Van Gogh était fou.

Saint-Rémy-des-Alpilles, 18 septembre 1949

Anoukis and later Jeanne

I shall reveal you to those I love, like a lasting flash of summer-lightning, without any explanation, just as you appeared to me that day, Jeanne, when, as morning plied to your plan, you led us on from rock to rock up to the self-fulfilment that we call a summit. With your face half-hidden in the crook of your arm and your fingers clutching at your shoulder, you rewarded us for climbing so high with a town, with the sufferings and the name of a tutelary spirit, with the abandoned stretches of a wasteland, and with the cautious curve of a river on whose banks builders stood pondering. But I ran back to you, Sickle, for you were burning the offering made to you. And neither time, nor beauty nor heart-unbridling chance could compare with you.

So I resurrected my ancient treasures, our common wealth, and overriding thoughts of what tomorrow will destroy, I remembered that you were both Anoukis the Embracer and also, marvellously, inexplicably, Jeanne, my best friend's sister – just as, without any explanation, you were the Strange One in the mind of that poor old bell-ringer whose father used to go about muttering that Van Gogh was mad.

Saint-Rémy-des-Alpilles, 18 September 1949

Recours au ruisseau

Sur l'aire du courant, dans les joncs agités, j'ai retracé ta ville. Les maçons au large feutre sont venus; ils se sont appliqués à suivre mon mouvement. Ils ne concevaient pas ma construction. Leur compétence s'alarmait.

Je leur ai dit que, confiante, tu attendais proche de là que j'eusse atteint la demie de ma journée pour connaître mon travail. À ce moment, notre satisfaction commune l'effacerait, nous le recommencerions plus haut, identiquement, dans la certitude de notre amour. Railleurs, ils se sont écartés. Je voyais, tandis qu'ils remettaient leur veste de toile, le gravier qui brillait dans le ciel du ruisseau et dont je n'avais, moi, nul besoin.

Recourse to the river

On the stream's surface, amidst the wind-swept rushes, I redesigned your town. The masons in their wide-brimmed felt hats arrived; they strove to understand what I was trying to do. They could make no sense of what I was building. They felt their competence was being attacked.

I told them that you believed in me and were waiting nearby until I had done a half-day's work before you came to inspect my work. That our shared delight would then erase it all, that we would start again on a higher plane, but in the same way, certain of the reality of our love. Laughing at me, the masons started to leave. As they were putting on their canvas jackets, I could see the gravel sparkling in the sky of the stream and knew that I had no need of it.

Le masque funèbre

Il était un homme, une fois, qui n'ayant plus faim, plus jamais faim, tant il avait dévoré d'héritages, englouti d'aliments, appauvri son prochain, trouva sa table vide, son lit désert, sa femme grosse, et la terre mauvaise dans le champ de son cœur.

N'ayant pas de tombeau et se voulant en vie, n'ayant rien à donner et moins à recevoir, les objets le fuyant, les bêtes lui mentant, il vola la famine et s'en fit une assiette qui devint son miroir et sa propre déroute.

The sun turns; image of the lamb, it is already a funerary mask.

The funerary mask

Once upon a time there was a man who no longer had any desire to eat because he had so greedily devoured legacies, wolfed food and made his neighbours poor that he found his table bare, his bed empty, his wife pregnant, and the ground barren in the field of his heart.

Having no tomb and wishing to go on living, having nothing to give and even less to receive, avoided by things, lied to by animals, he stole famine and made of it a platter that became his mirror and his personal catastrophe.

Les lichens

Je marchais parmi les bosses d'une terre écurée, les haleines secrètes, les plantes sans mémoire. La montagne se levait, flacon empli d'ombre qu'étreignait par instant le geste de la soif. Ma trace, mon existence se perdaient. Ton visage glissait à reculons devant moi. Ce n'était qu'une tache à la recherche de l'abeille qui la ferait fleur et la dirait vivante. Nous allions nous séparer. Tu demeurerais sur le plateau des arômes et je pénétrerais dans le jardin du vide. Là, sous la sauvegarde des rochers, dans la plénitude du vent, je demanderais à la nuit véritable de disposer de mon sommeil pour accroître ton bonheur. Et tous les fruits t'appartiendraient.

The lichens

I was walking through the bosses of a scoured land, through its secret breathings and its amnesic plants. The mountain rose up before me, a shadow-filled flask caressed now and then by the gesture of thirst. My trace and my existence were fading. Your face was gliding ahead of me and looking back. It was just a speck in search of the bee that would make it a flower and say it was alive. We were going to part. You would remain on the high aromatic plateau and I would plunge down into the garden of emptiness. There, protected by the rocks, in the fullness of the wind, I would ask the true night to use my sleep to increase your happiness. And all fruits would then belong to you.

JOUE ET DORS

PLAY AND SLEEP

Joue et dors...

Joue et dors, bonne soif, nos oppresseurs ici ne sont pas sévères.
Volontiers ils plaisantent ou nous tiennent le bras
Pour traverser la périlleuse saison.
Sans doute, le poison s'est-il assoupi en eux,
Au point de desserrer leur barbare humeur.
Comme ils nous ont pourtant pourchassés jusqu'ici, ma soif,
Et contraints à vivre dans l'abandon de notre amour réduit à une
    mortelle providence!
Aromates, est-ce pour vous? Ou toutes plantes qui luttez sous un
    mur de sécheresse, est-ce pour vous? Ou nuages au grand large,
    prenant congé de la colonne?
Dans l'immense, comment deviner?

Qu'entreprendre pour fausser compagnie à ces tyrans, ô mon amie?
Joue et dors, que je mesure bien nos chances.
Mais, si tu me viens en aide, je devrais t'entraîner avec moi, et je ne
    veux pas t'exposer.
Alors, restons encore...Et qui pourrait nous dire lâches?

Play and sleep...

Play and sleep, good thirst, our oppressors here are not harsh.
They enjoy joking or holding our arms
To help us cross the perilous season.
The poison is clearly dulled in them,
Even their barbaric mood is unclenched.
And yet how they have always hunted us down, my thirst,
And forced us to live in renunciation of our love which was reduced
    to an arid salvation!
Aromatic herbs, is all this for your sake? Or all you plants struggling
    under a wall of dryness, is it for your sake? Or for you, clouds
    that leave the column and sail off?
Faced with infinity, how can we guess?

What can we do to give these tyrants the slip, O my beloved?
Sleep and play, while I calculate our chances.
But, if you come to my aid, I would have to take you with me, and
    I don't want to expose you to risks.
So, let us stay here for a while... And who could call us cowards?

Centon

Vous recherchez mon point faible, ma faille? Sa découverte vous permettrait de m'avoir à merci? Mais, assaillant, ne voyez-vous pas que je suis un crible et que votre peu de cervelle sèche parmi mes rayons expirés?

Je n'ai ni chaud ni froid: je gouverne. Cependant n'allongez pas trop la main vers le sceptre de mon pouvoir. Il glace, il brûle... Vous en éventeriez la sensation.

J'aime, je capture et je rends à quelqu'un. Je suis dard et j'abreuve de lumière le prisonnier de la fleur. Tels sont mes contradictions, mes services.

En ce temps, je souriais au monde et le monde me souriait. En ce temps qui ne fut jamais et que je lis dans la poussière.

Ceux qui regardent souffrir le lion dans sa cage pourrissent dans la mémoire du lion.

Un roi qu'un coureur de chimère rattrape, je lui souhaite d'en mourir.

Cento

Are you looking for my weak point, for my flaw? If you found it, would that put me at your mercy? But, attacker, can't you see that I am a riddle and that your few grey cells dry out when caught in my dead wires?

I am neither cold nor hot: I govern. However don't stretch out your hand too eagerly to touch the sceptre of my power. It chills, it burns... You would empty it of all sensation.

I love, I capture and I repay someone. I am a bee-sting and I drench the flower's prisoner with light. Such are my contradictions and my duties.

At that time, I smiled at the world and the world smiled at me. At that time which never existed and which I read in the dust.

Those who watch the lion suffer in his cage rot in the lion's memory.

I think that every king caught by a chaser after rainbows deserves to die.

Les inventeurs

Ils sont venus, les forestiers de l'autre versant, les inconnus de nous,
les rebelles à nos usages.
Ils sont venus nombreux.
Leur troupe est apparue à la ligne de partage des cèdres
Et du champ de la vieille moisson désormais irrigué et vert.
La longue marche les avait échauffés.
Leur casquette cassait sur leurs yeux et leur pied fourbu se posait
dans le vague.
Ils nous ont aperçus et se sont arrêtés.
Visiblement ils ne présumaient pas nous trouver là,
Sur des terres faciles et des sillons bien clos,
Tout à fait insouciants d'une audience.
Nous avons levé le front et les avons encouragés.

Le plus disert s'est approché, puis un second tout aussi déraciné et
lent.
Nous sommes venus, dirent-ils, vous prévenir de l'arrivée prochaine
de l'ouragan, de votre implacable adversaire.
Pas plus que vous, nous ne le connaissons
Autrement que par des relations et des confidences d'ancêtres.
Mais pourquoi sommes-nous heureux incompréhensiblement devant
vous et soudain pareils à des enfants?

Nous avons dit merci et les avons congédiés.
Mais auparavant ils ont bu, et leurs mains tremblaient, et leurs yeux
riaient sur les bords.
Hommes d'arbres et de cognée, capables de tenir tête à quelque
terreur, mais inaptes à conduire l'eau, à aligner des bâtisses, à les
enduire de couleurs plaisantes,
Ils ignoreraient le jardin d'hiver et l'économie de la joie.

Certes, nous aurions pu les convaincre et les conquérir,
Car l'angoisse de l'ouragan est émouvante.
Oui, l'ouragan allait bientôt venir;
Mais cela valait-il la peine que l'on en parlât et qu'on dérangeât
l'avenir?
Là où nous sommes, il n'y a pas de crainte urgente.

Sivergues, 30 septembre 1949

The inventors

They came, the foresters from the other side of the hill, men unknown to us and hostile to our ways.
They came in great numbers.
Their band appeared at the dividing line between the cedars
And the long-since harvested field which will now be watered and grow green.
Their long walk had made them hot and tired.
Their caps were pulled down over their eyes and their exhausted feet found no firm ground.
They caught sight of us and stopped.
Clearly they did not expect to find us there,
On friable land, amidst well-turned furrows,
Untroubled by the thought that they might be watched.
We looked up and beckoned to them.

Their best speaker came forward, then another, who was just as uprooted and slow.
'We have come,' they said, 'to warn you of the imminent arrival of your implacable foe, the hurricane.
Our knowledge of it, like yours, is gleaned only
From the tales and secrets told us by our old folk.
But why are we strangely happy here with you and suddenly like children?'

We thanked them and sent them on their way.
But first they drank wine, and their hands trembled, and the corners of their eyes puckered in laughter.
Foresters and fellers, able to face up to unknown terrors yet unable to divert a stream, to align a building or to paint it in pretty colours,
They could know nothing of winter gardens or the economy of joy.

Certainly, we could have convinced and conquered them,
For the dread of the hurricane makes everyone shiver.
And yes, the hurricane was about to arrive;
But was this worth mentioning, was it worth disturbing the future?
Here in our region, there are no pressing fears.

Sivergues, 30 September 1949

Les seigneurs de Maussane

L'un après l'autre, ils ont voulu nous prédire un avenir heureux,
Avec une éclipse à leur image et toute l'angoisse conforme à nous.
Nous avons dédaigné cette égalité,
Répondu non à leurs mots assidus.
Nous avons suivi l'empierrement que notre cœur s'était tracé,
Jusqu'aux plaines de l'air et l'unique silence.
Nous avons fait saigner notre amour exigeant,
Lutter notre bonheur avec chaque caillou.

Ils disent à présent qu'au-delà de leur vue,
La grêle les effraie plus que la neige des morts!

The Lords of Maussane

One after another, they sought to predict a happy future for us,
With an eclipse in their image and all anguish made for us.
We chose to scorn this equality,
Said no to their entreaties.
We followed the metalled road traced by our hearts
Up to the airy plains where silence reigns.
We made our demanding love bleed,
Made our happiness fight with every stone.

Now they say that, beyond their ken, beyond their sight,
The hail frightens them more than the snows of the dead!

Pleinement

Quand nos os eurent touché terre,
Croulant à travers nos visages,
Mon amour, rien ne fut fini.
Un amour frais vint dans un cri
Nous ranimer et nous reprendre.
Et si la chaleur s'était tue,
La chose qui continuait,
Opposée à la vie mourante,
À l'infini s'élaborait.
Ce que nous avions vu flotter
Bord à bord avec la douleur
Était là comme dans un nid,
Et ses deux yeux nous unissaient
Dans un naissant consentement.
La mort n'avait pas grandi
Malgré des laines ruisselantes,
Et le bonheur pas commencé
A l'ecoute de nos présences;
L'herbe était nue et piétinée.

Fully

When our bones had come to earth,
Crumbling through our faces,
O my love, nothing was ended.
A fresh new love came in a cry
To revive and repossess us.
And if warmth had fallen silent,
The continuity of presence,
Ever hostile to dying life,
Was moving its way towards infinity.
What we had seen float and drift
Beside and with suffering
Was now present as if in a nest,
And its two eyes united us
In a nascent consent, in a yes.
Death had gained no stature
Though our wool was still unwoven,
And our happiness not attuned
To the music of our presence.
The grass was naked and trampled.

Rougeur des Matinaux

À Henry Mathieu

La vérité est personnelle.

Prenez garde: tous ne sont pas dignes de la confidence.

Accolade à celui qui, émergeant de sa fatigue et de sa sueur, s'avancera et me dira: «Je suis venu pour te tromper.»

Ô grande barre noire, en route vers ta mort, pourquoi serait-ce toujours à toi de montrer l'éclair?

I

L'état d'esprit du soleil levant est allégresse malgré le jour cruel et le souvenir de la nuit. La teinte du caillot devient la rougeur de l'aurore.

II

Quand on a mission d'éveiller, on commence par faire sa toilette dans la rivière. Le premier enchantement comme le premier saisissement sont pour soi.

III

Impose ta chance, serre ton bonheur et va vers ton risque. À te regarder, *ils* s'habitueront.

IV

Au plus fort de l'orage, il y a toujours un oiseau pour nous rassurer. C'est l'oiseau inconnu. Il chante avant de s'envoler.

Redness of the Dawnbreakers

For Henry Mathieu

Truth is personal.

Be careful: not everyone deserves to be trusted with your secrets.

I shall embrace the man who, emerging wearily from his toils, advances to tell me: 'I have come to deceive you.'

O great black bar heading towards your death, why should it always be you who points to the flash of lightning?

I

The rising sun is joyful despite the cruel light of day and the memory of the night. The colour of the blood-clot becomes the redness of the dawn.

II

When your duty is to waken others, you start the day by washing in the river. The first moment of delight and the first rush of emotion are yours alone.

III

Trust firmly in your luck, cling to your happiness and dare to take risks. *They* will see you and learn to accept you.

IV

When the storm is at its fiercest, there is always a bird to reassure us. An unknown bird – who sings before flying off.

143

V

La sagesse est de ne pas s'agglomérer, mais, dans la création et dans la nature communes, de trouver notre nombre, notre réciprocité, nos différences, notre passage, notre vérité, et ce peu de désespoir qui en est l'aiguillon et le mouvant brouillard.

VI

Allez à l'essentiel: n'avez-vous pas besoin de jeunes arbres pour reboiser votre forêt?

VII

L'intensité est silencieuse. Son image ne l'est pas. (J'aime qui m'éblouit puis accentue l'obscur à l'interieur de moi.)

VIII

Combien souffre ce monde, pour devenir celui de l'homme, d'être façonné entre les quatre murs d'un livre! Qu'il soit ensuite remis aux mains de spéculateurs et d'extravagants qui le pressent d'avancer plus vite que son propre mouvement, comment ne pas voir là plus que de la malchance? Combattre vaille que vaille cette fatalité à l'aide de sa magie, ouvrir dans l'aile de la route, de ce qui en tient lieu, d'insatiables randonnées, c'est la tâche des Matinaux. La mort n'est qu'un sommeil entier et pur avec le signe plus qui le pilote et l'aide à fendre le flot du devenir. Qu'as-tu à t'alarmer de ton état alluvial? Cesse de prendre la branche pour le tronc et la racine pour le vide. C'est un petit commencement.

IX

Il faut souffler sur quelques lueurs pour faire de la bonne lumière. Beaux yeux brûlés parachèvent le don.

Wisdom comes not from huddling together but from discovering, in our similarity and shared creativity, how numerous we are, how we respond to each other, how different we all are, how we pass through life, what our truth is – and from discovering the grain of despair which is its goad and swirling fog.

VI

Go to the heart of the matter: don't you need young trees if you want to replant your forest?

VII

Intensity is silent. Its image is not. (I love everything that dazzles me and then accentuates the darkness within me.)

VIII

How this world suffers from being crushed between the four walls of a book in order to become the world of men! If it is then placed in the hands of speculators and madmen who force it to advance faster than it should go, isn't this more than mere bad luck? Fighting – come what may – against this doom with the help of its magic, opening up insatiable walks in the replacement-road's wing: this is the task of the Dawnbreakers. Death is merely a pure and absolute sleep with a plus sign piloting it and aiding it to cleave through the tide of becoming. Why should you be alarmed by its alluvial state? Stop taking the branch for the trunk and the root for the void. That is a first step.

IX

You must blow on embers if you want to create true light. Beautiful scorched eyes make the gift perfect.

X

Femelle redoutable, elle porte la rage dans sa morsure et un froid mortel dans ses flancs, cette connaissance qui, partie d'une noble ambition, finit par trouver sa mesure dans nos larmes et dans notre jugulation. Ne vous méprenez pas, ô vous entre les meilleurs dont elle convoite le bras et guette la défaillance.

XI

À toute pression de rompre avec nos chances, notre morale, et de nous soumettre à tel modèle simplificateur, ce qui ne doit rien à l'homme, mais nous veut du bien, nous exhorte: «Insurgé, insurgé, insurgé...»

XII

L'aventure personnelle, l'aventure prodiguée, communauté de nos aurores.

XIII

Conquête et conservation indéfinie de cette conquête *en avant de nous* qui murmure notre naufrage, déroute notre déception.

XIV

Nous avons cette particularité parfois de nous balancer en marchant. Le temps nous est léger, le sol nous est facile, notre pied ne tourne qu'à bon escient.

XV

Quand nous disons: *le cœur* (et le disons à regret), il s'agit du cœur attisant que recouvre la chair miraculeuse et commune, et qui peut à chaque instant cesser de battre et d'accorder.

X

Knowledge is fearsomely female: when it bites, it infects us with rabid rage, but it also clutches us between its thighs in a chilling embrace. Our search for knowledge may be noble, but it will always lead to tears and strangulation. Be aware of this all you whose belief and weakness Knowledge will exploit.

XI

Whenever we are pressured to break with our possibilities and moral standards and to submit to some simplifying model, the force which owes nothing to man but which does wish us well, exhorts us: 'Rebel, rebel, rebel...'

XII

Personal experiences, unstinting experiences, convergence of our dawns.

XIII

The conquest and the shaky maintaining of that conquest *ahead of us* which murmurs our shipwreck makes us worry about other things.

XIV

One of our characteristics is that we sometimes sway as we walk. For us, time is fluid and the earth is easy; our feet turn only when they should.

XV

When we say *the heart* (and say it longingly), we are speaking of the inflaming heart which, hidden under shared and miraculous flesh, can at any moment stop beating and giving.

XVI

Entre *ton* plus grand bien et *leur* moindre mal rougeoie la poésie.

XVII

L'essaim, l'éclair et l'anathème, trois obliques d'un même sommet.

XVIII

Se tenir fermement sur terre, et, avec amour, donner le bras à un fruit non accepté de ceux qui vous appuient, édifier ce qu'on croit sa maison, sans le concours de la première pierre qui toujours inconcevablement fera faute, c'est *la malédiction*.

XIX

Ne te plains pas de vivre plus près de la mort que les mortels.

XX

Il semble que l'on naît toujours à mi-chemin du commencement et de la fin du monde. Nous grandissons en révolte ouverte presque aussi furieusement contre ce qui nous entraîne que contre ce qui nous retient.

XXI

Imite le moins possible les hommes dans leur énigmatique maladie de faire des nœuds.

XXII

La mort n'est haïssable que parce qu'elle affecte séparément chacun de nos cinq sens, puis tous à la fois. À la rigueur, l'ouïe la négligerait.

XVI

It is between *your* greater good and *their* lesser evil that poetry glows.

XVII

The swarm, the lightning-flash and the anathema: three slopes of the same mountain-top.

XVIII

To stand firmly planted on the earth and lovingly to give your arm to a fruit rejected by those who support you, to build what you think is your house without the aid of the foundation stone which for some reason will always be missing: that is mankind's curse.

XIX

Do not complain that you live closer to death than mortal people.

XX

It seems that we are born half-way between the beginning and the end of the world. We grow in open revolt almost as furiously against what draws us onward as against what holds us back.

XXI

Imitate as little as possible those who are obsessed with tying knots.

XXII

Death is hateful only because it affects each of our five senses one by one, and then all together. Hearing might just possibly forget about death.

XXIII

On ne bâtit *multiformément* que sur l'erreur. C'est ce qui nous permet de nous supposer, à chaque renouveau, heureux.

XXIV

Quand le navire s'engloutit, sa voiture se sauve à l'intérieur de nous. Elle mâte sur notre sang. Sa neuve impatience se concentre pour d'autres obstinés voyages. N'est-ce pas, vous, qui êtes aveugle sur la mer? Vous qui vacillez dans tout ce bleu, ô tristesse dressée aux vagues les plus loin?

XXV

Nous sommes des passants *appliqués* à passer, donc à jeter le trouble, à infliger notre chaleur, à dire notre exubérance. Voilà pourquoi nous intervenons! Voilà pourquoi nous sommes intempestifs et insolites! Notre aigrette n'y est rien. Notre utilité est tournée contre l'employeur.

XXVI

Je puis désespérer de moi et garder mon espoir en Vous. Je suis tombé de mon éclat, et la mort vue de tous, vous ne la marquez pas, fougère dans le mur, promeneuse à mon bras.

XXVII

Enfin, si tu détruis, que ce soit avec des outils nuptiaux.

XXIII

We build – *in a many-sided way* – only on our mistakes. That is why whenever we repeat them, we can convince ourselves that we are happy.

XXIV

When the ship founders, its rigging flies off, penetrating us and masting on our blood. Newly impatient, the rigging prepares for other obstinate voyages. Is this not so, you who are blind on the sea? You who vacillate in all this blue, O sadness erected on the most distant waves?

XXV

We are passers-by *determined* to pass by and so to cause trouble, to inflict our warmth, to express our exuberance. That is why we intervene! And why we are untimely and strange! Our aigrette means nothing here. Our usefulness is turned against those who exploit it.

XXVI

I can despair of myself and maintain my hope in You. I have fallen from my heights of brightness but you, fern in the wall, my faithful companion, you never let anyone know that you've witnessed the death everyone else has seen.

XXVII

In short, if you do destroy, let it be with nuptial tools.

Ils sont privilégiés…

Ils sont privilégiés ceux que le soleil et le vent suffisent à rendre fous, sont suffisants à saccager!

Pourquoi se rendre?

Oh! Rencontrée, nos ailes vont côte à côte
Et l'azur leur est fidèle.
Mais qu'est-ce qui brille encore au-dessus de nous?

Le reflet mourant de notre audace.
Lorsque nous l'aurons parcouru,
Nous n'affligerons plus la terre:
Nous nous regarderons.

Privileged are those…

Privileged are those who can be driven mad and devastated by the sun and the wind!

Why surrender?

Oh! Encountered One, our wings fly side by side
And the azure sky is faithful to them.
But what is that still shining above us?

The dying reflection of our daring.
When we have crossed it
We shall no longer trouble the earth:
We shall look at each other.

Toute vie…

Toute vie qui doit poindre
achève un blessé.
Voici l'arme,
rien,
vous, moi, réversiblement
ce livre,
et l'énigme
qu'à votre tour vous deviendrez
dans le caprice amer des sables.

Every life…

Each new life about to dawn
kills a wounded man.
This is the weapon,
nothing,
you, I, reversibly
this book,
and the riddle
which you in turn will become
in the bitter caprice of the sands.

Bloodaxe Contemporary French Poets

Series Editors: Timothy Mathews & Michael Worton

FRENCH-ENGLISH BILINGUAL EDITIONS

1: **Yves Bonnefoy:** *On the Motion and Immobility of Douve /*
   Du mouvement et de l'immobilité de Douve
   Trans. Galway Kinnell. Introduction: Timothy Mathews. £12

2: **René Char:** *The Dawn Breakers / Les Matinaux*
   Trans. & intr. Michael Worton. £12

3: **Henri Michaux:** *Spaced, Displaced / Déplacements Dégagements*
   Trans. David & Helen Constantine. Introduction: Peter Broome. £12

4: **Aimé Césaire:** *Notebook of a Return to My Native Land /*
   Cahier d'un retour au pays natal
   Trans. & intr. Mireille Rosello (with Annie Pritchard). £12

5: **Philippe Jaccottet:** *Under Clouded Skies / Beauregard*
   Pensées sous les nuages / Beauregard
   Trans. David Constantine & Mark Treharne.
   Introduction: Mark Treharne. £12

6: **Paul Éluard:** *Unbroken Poetry II / Poésie ininterrompue II*
   Trans. Gilbert Bowen. Introduction: Jill Lewis. £12

7: **André Frénaud:** *Rome the Sorceress / La Sorcière de Rome*
   Trans. Keith Bosley. Introduction: Peter Broome. £8.95

8: **Gérard Macé:** *Wood Asleep / Bois dormant*
   Trans. David Kelley. Introduction: Jean-Pierre Richard. £8.95

9: **Guillevic:** *Carnac*
   Trans. John Montague. Introduction: Stephen Romer. £12

10: **Salah Stétié:** *Cold Water Shielded: Selected Poems*
    Trans. & intr. Michael Bishop. £9.95

'Bloodaxe's Contemporary French Poets series could not have arrived at a more opportune time, and I cannot remember any translation initiative in the past thirty years that has been more ambitious or more coherently planned in its attempt to bring French poetry across the Channel and the Atlantic. Under the editorship of Timothy Mathews and Michael Worton, the series has a clear format and an even clearer sense of mission' – MALCOLM BOWIE, *TLS*